COURSE CORRECTED

It's not a Pivot. It's Your Path.

Featuring Marta Sauret Greca

Foreword by Dr. Shellie Hipsky

With stories by Jennie Askins, Heather Cherry,
Dorothy L. Clear, Lisa Fera, Jillian Forsberg,
Christine Furman, Denise Ann Galloni, Angela Goodman,
Tina Johnson, Judi Logan, Sheri Mancini, Leslie Pasco,
Sally Power, and Denise Stiffler

Stories Collected by Cori Wamsley

Aurora Corialis Publishing

Pittsburgh, PA

COURSE CORRECTED

Printed in the United States of America

Edited by: Allison Hrip, Aurora Corialis Publishing

Cover Design: Karen Captline, BetterBe Creative

Paperback ISBN: 978-1-958481-56-1

Ebook ISBN: 978-1-958481-57-8

Praise for Course Corrected

"This isn't a feel good book. It's a reckoning. Gentle in some places, guttural in others. These women didn't just survive collapse. They walked through it awake. Each story is a threshold. One you'll recognize if you've ever found yourself stripped down by grief, guided by God, and somehow still standing. If you've been brought to your knees, this book will speak to you. Not to fix you. But to remind you that the fire didn't end you. It re-formed you."

Amanda Kunkel
Universe Liaison

"*Course Corrected* is proof that hope, faith, timing, resilience, and love for oneself, and God, will always prevail. Knowing our worth and that we are here to love and help support each other is powerful. God's timing may not be ours, but ultimately, his timing is perfect. This book will help you feel that."

Dina Russo
Stroll Treesdale | Be Local

"*Course Corrected* is a powerful collection of stories that left me feeling seen, inspired, and motivated to take bold action in my own journey. Each chapter offers a unique lens on growth, resilience, and finding purpose—even through uncertainty. I'm walking away feeling reminded that we don't need permission to begin, we can decide to quiet the doubt and trust our own voice."

Kelly Featheringham, ACC
CEO | Team Leadership Solutions

"This book is a powerful blend of insight, inspiration, and practical guidance. Whether you're just beginning your journey or seeking a deeper transformation, it delivers exactly what you need."

Dr. Shanea Clancy, DNP, EMBA-H, RN, CARN-AP, FIAAN
President & Founder | Clancy Consulting Services

"So many women are on a quest to making more meaningful connections or 'find their tribe.' These collected stories actually create that sense of community in such a poignant and diverse way. The demonstration of strength and courage from each account has the power to cultivate, within the reader, their own recognition of empowerment. We often lessen, ignore, or forget our own setbacks, struggles, challenges, and tragedies and how our resilience and determination helped us overcome. But this book is not just about bouncing back, but about adapting, accepting, and nurturing the spirit of courage within all of us—a spirit that has the ability to inspire and uplift others."

Kym Gable
Anchor/Reporter

"*Course Corrected* is a heart-filled, inspiring collection of stories from women who faced life-altering challenges and chose to rise stronger.

"Each personal narrative reveals how these women found strength to course correct, realign with purpose, and design impactful lives for their families, businesses, and communities. The stories are authentic, relatable, and filled with hope.

"I especially love how real and vulnerable the stories are, showing that success isn't about avoiding obstacles but facing them with intention and courage. The writing style kept me engaged from start to finish, and each journey felt personal and transformative.

"If you're seeking real stories of strength, clarity, and hope—you'll find them here. I highly recommend reading this collection—it's an uplifting and empowering guide for anyone navigating life's unexpected turns.

Deborah Leben
CEO & Founder | DL Coaching & Career Successes Academy

"*Course Corrected* is a collection of stories that truly reveals the power of what happens when dark moments collide with growth and perspective. Sometimes, there's more to learn than lose. Don't overlook the encouragement of Heather Cherry or the strength of Angela Goodman—both shine brightly in this moving anthology."

Kaila Amariah
Actress and Film Editor

"This is a truly inspirational and uplifting collection of stories told by women for... really anyone. Each woman has endured life-changing events, many of which were not expected, and found their way through the hardest times of their lives to the other side, not just surviving, but flourishing.

"Every journey is unique, and uniquely told, but every story will leave you in tears, cheering on the writer, and best of all, feeling inspired and ready to face your own personal challenges with love and positivity."

Mona Shroff
Author

"*Course Corrected* is a powerful message with raw courage, divine redemption, and unrelenting faith. This book is not just a collection of stories—it's a lifeline for anyone navigating the moments of life when doors close and answers are few.

"As someone who has dedicated my life to helping people fulfill their purpose, I can say with confidence: this book will stir your soul, renew your faith, and reignite your hope. Whether you're in a valley or on a mountaintop, this book will remind you that setbacks are not the end of the story—they're the beginning of your transformation.

"I highly recommend *Course Corrected* to anyone who needs to be reminded that they are never alone—and that their greatest breakthrough may be just one course correction away."

Jeff Hancher
President and Founder | Jeff Hancher Enterprsies

"This anthology is a powerful celebration of resilience, strength, and the diverse voices of women who inspire change. Each story resonates with authenticity and courage, offering a rich tapestry of empowerment and hope at times when life is challenging. The collection uplifts and motivates, reminding readers of the collective power found in shared experiences. It's a deeply moving and essential read for anyone seeking inspiration from women who lead with heart and have the power to overcome any obstacles in life."

Lisa Vidakovic
Physical Therapist & Founder | Wellness Collaborative

"Course Corrected is a lovely collection of inspirational stories from courageous and resilient women. They remind us that it's never too late to reinvent ourselves. That our dreams can come true with determination and perseverance. To keep going and never look back. These are some badass women!"

Darlene (Charlee) Bridger

"I appreciated the opportunity to read fifteen stories of lives of strong, powerful, intelligent women, determined not to be left behind by fate, dire circumstances, or indecision. Their different stories of how they made course corrections that altered their very being are simple, straight forward, rigorously honest, and encouraging to any woman at most stages of their travels through life as we know it today.

"I especially was touched by the changes brought about by those who were open minded, willing to hear and try different ideas and approaches to problem solving, stepping into a different skin or at least trying to do something a new way. Asking for help. Admitting something was wrong in their lives. Being willing to change, even if it was in baby steps, especially as they were dealing with intense pain—physical, emotional, spiritual, or all.

"It was encouraging to read all of them. Bless these women for sharing their courageous ways."

Rosemarie Fox McShane, MA
Counselor and Poet

"*Course Corrected* is a powerful collection of stories written by courageous women who turned life's detours into divine direction. Each chapter is a testimony of faith, perseverance, and transformation. Judi Logan's contribution especially stands out—a heartfelt reminder of the "BUT GOD" moments that change everything. This book is more than a read; it's a source of encouragement, healing, and hope for anyone navigating life's unexpected turns. A true must-read for those who believe in second chances, miracles, and the perfect timing of God's plan."

Kimberly Starr
Environmental Engineer | Entrepreneur | Mary Kay National Sales Director Emeritus | Founder at Three International | Empowering Dreams Through Leadership and Innovation

Table of Contents

Foreword

Dr. Shellie Hipsky

"When one door closes, another opens." It's such a common phrase. But what happens in that hallway—the often dark, uncertain space in between the doors—can show us our true strength. *Course Corrected* is not just a collection of stories compiled by Marta Sauret Greca; it is a sacred map—a guidebook of grace, grit, and unshakable faith in the face of adversity.

As a woman who has been through the fire more than once and come out stronger and better, not broken, I know the courage it takes to pivot. To walk away from what no longer serves your soul. Whether that be a toxic relationship, the way you once defined yourself, or a rock bottom scenario, sometimes you must simply surrender what is "comfortable" and move toward what is calling you. This book is an impactful tribute to those bold steps.

In these pages, you will meet women who stood at the edge of trauma, betrayal, loss, fear—and chose to rise. Women who listened not to the noise of the world, but to the divine whisper within. Each story in *Course Corrected* is a beacon of hope, a celebration of transformation, and a reminder that sometimes, our most painful moments become the birthplace of our purpose.

As the founder of the Global Sisterhood 501 (c)(3) nonprofit, which helps women and children worldwide, and someone who has had the honor of spotlighting thousands of women's stories from across the globe through multiple media, I can tell you this with certainty: Empowered women can empower the world. And when women come together to share their truths with vulnerability and strength, mountains move. Chains break. Futures shift.

So please, let this anthology speak to your heart. Let it remind you that inside every ending is the seed of a beautiful new beginning. It is our intent that the stories within these moving chapters encourage you to keep rising even on the darkest of days. We want you to know that something extraordinary is waiting on the other side of your faith.

To the brave authors of this impactful anthology, we thank you for your authenticity, your courage, and your light.

To the women reading this, know you are not alone. Your path is divine. And your rise is inevitable.

With love and a fierce belief in your journey,

Dr. Shellie Hipsky

CEO of Inspiring Lives International, Executive Director of the Global Sisterhood, and Author of Fifteen International Bestselling Books

https://www.globalsisterhoodonline.org/

Introduction

Marta Sauret Greca

You know that moment when you decide you're going to be your own savior, and you're going to stop waiting for someone to give you a chance, and instead, create the opportunities for yourself? That was what happened for me.

I already had five kids, and I was doing the hustle, but my workload didn't match my bank account. So, like many entrepreneurs around that time, I sought the help of business mentors and coaches, and I grew my businesses to financial heights I could have never imagined. For years after, my revenue stream was beautiful, and I got to be a full-time mom to my kids, working whenever I felt like it while making a generous income for my family almost literally in my sleep. We aimed toward our dream home on a little lake and were able to move into it. Big things were happening for my husband in the land development space, and our marriage felt stronger than ever. Simultaneously, life was so good that we decided to have another baby, which was deeply on my heart. All was well with my soul.

And then, the beautiful house of cards I had built around me started to topple down one by one. My mom, who was also my best friend, received an end-of-life diagnosis and passed away. Shortly after, my dad was diagnosed with Alzheimer's, necessitating big moves and changes. In the years following, we faced significant turbulence and insecurity in my husband's land development endeavors that affected everything. I struggled with two miscarriages, and my grandmother passed away as well. My mojo to maintain a thriving business was gone, and the revenue decline matched my energy. I started to wonder if this was self-sabotage or divine intervention or if I had manifested all of this somehow.

All I had the energy for was to be in my feminine energy (in the metaphysical sense), be present for my family, and attract the clients I loved who would naturally come to me. Although working with these incredible clients was still a six-figure-plus revenue, it paled in comparison to the financial levels (the height and caliber) of the team and business I'd built, and a family of now eight, which would soon be nine. Something inexplicable was tugging at me, so I let my business as I knew it go and started anew.

In these moments of perceived human decline, I learned deep, humble lessons that led me through the story I share in my chapter of this book. During this time, I found myself getting caught up in actions and thoughts that were fear-based and scarcity-minded. I had to continuously redirect my energy and mindset toward shifts of divine truth that made my faith stronger than ever before. I infused fun and light wherever I could in a playful way. But what really helped get me through these times was reading, listening, and witnessing stories of failure from massively, wildly, unimaginably successful people who became even higher versions of themselves *because* of these experiences of loss. I would intentionally show my brain these stories as divine truths when my brain—doing what the brain does in trying to protect us—could only compute and output negative realities. Reading these stories, I was telling my brain: *Thank you for sharing this worst-case scenario you've concocted, brain, and trying to protect me, but here are some wonderful scenarios that could ALSO come from all of this ...*"

So it only seemed natural that when Aurora Corialis Publishing approached me for a book project, I would gather a group of women together to share their stories of trials and tribulations transformed into passion and purpose through God's divine path for each of us. We were all course corrected in this book. So let the stories from the amazing women in this book unfold before you as reminders that only God knows what's truly meant for you, and everything that is happening *to* you could be happening *for* you. That's a hard truth to hear if you're going through a tough time, but it's also comforting to know that there are guardian angels out there conspiring *for* you, whether you know it or not.

During the personal experiences I reference here, I remember vividly standing on my back deck, overlooking our little lake and firmly speaking out, demanding an explanation, "God, why are you putting me through this?!" And I still get chills when I think of the answer I felt in return. It was almost as if I'd heard it audibly, *My daughter, don't you know that this is all FOR you?* In that moment, I remembered that I have always been provided for, sometimes in the most miraculous and magical ways, and that I would always be divinely guided and supported, whether I can recognize it or not.

May this book be a reminder to you that you will also always be divinely provided for, and may every chapter be a burst of positivity, boosting you higher and higher into the most luxuriously peaceful vibrations. May you thoroughly enjoy the experience.

Course Corrected

Marta Sauret Greca

What if your biggest fear came true and it turned out to be the thing that propelled you forward toward your destined divine path? I'm not saying that's the case every time. I certainly wish that *my* worst fear hadn't happened, but it did, and it has been my inspiration since day one of my current business. Because of it, I get to help so many families and business owners every single day.

This story is about that time I was giving birth to my sixth baby and found out my mom was dying at the same time.

———

There was a knock on the hospital room door, and we all looked at each other. We weren't expecting anybody else at the moment. We were at the bedside of my mother, who was within hours of passing. We compulsively watched the heart monitor and listened to its beeps that told us she was still alive. In her hospital bed, she lay peacefully sleeping. We had been told by doctors that this was it.

"You might want to come down. It's not going to be much longer now," were almost the exact words of my dad, who'd phoned me the day prior, but said in Italian. My dad is from France, and met my mom as an adult in Italy. They lived there together, had me and my four siblings, and then moved us to the United States when I was nine. We still speak Italian with our parents.

We were in this surreal time and space, knowing that within minutes (or hours), my mother's heart would beat its last heartbeat. We were experiencing a reality that didn't *feel* real at all until the knock on the door brought us back to truth—one that I had to face with a newborn baby in tow.

The night before, at this very same hospital, the staff discovered that I had brought my newborn baby boy into my mom's room. "This is fine for now. But you're going to need to figure something else out tomorrow," one of the nurses said matter-of-factly as she briefly popped her head into the room to deliver the message. I remember feeling confused yet amused by her statement, thinking sarcastically, *You mean if my mom doesn't die right away tonight, I'd better find a babysitter?*

Humor is a coping mechanism for me. I can see it in everything, and I often think that things will work out for me and often for the better. This time, it didn't.

When my mom received her end-of-life diagnosis, I thought she was going to be like one of those stories when someone's given two weeks to live, but they end up living for years. That wasn't the case for my mom. We did, within a few weeks of discovering her final cancer diagnosis, receive news that she had progressed significantly, and we moved her from the skilled nursing facility to a hospital when there was no other choice. She was going to die.

One of the only certain things in life is that we will pass. And it was time for my mom. She was ready. She had been suffering for a long time from many health complications. This time around, it was breast cancer that had metastasized into lung cancer and spread throughout her bones, causing her a significant amount of pain and difficulty breathing. Eventually, this transformed into difficulty for her to even exist.

Before that, she had beaten cancer twice, which gave us decades more with my mom. That time allowed her to start a family. It allowed her to have grandkids. She also had heart surgery to replace two heart valves, which gave her extra years with her loving family too.

She was a God-loving and -trusting woman. She had been through it and was prepared to go. She peacefully accepted her diagnosis and the fact that her life on earth with us was coming to completion.

As difficult as it was to accept this, she had expressed wanting to pass at home. However, in Pennsylvania, that is easier said than done. It is not something that is funded by your health insurance, unlike a skilled nursing facility, hospice, or a hospital. So, we had to choose for my mom to pass at a skilled nursing facility, but then had to move her to a hospital. I had just given birth at the same time as these diagnoses, so I was unable to care for her in my own home while juggling five other kids and healing from childbirth. I was even more incapable of caring for her in the comfort of her own home.

Furthermore, my dad was not able to care for her during her final days. We would realize soon after her passing that he was experiencing dementia, which made it hard for him to take care of himself, let alone another person. So here we were, in a hospital room, waiting for my mom to pass, with a baby in my baby carrier, smuggled in so I could be there both for my newborn and my passing mother, as well as my family and myself.

I had tried to abide by the hospital rules, by the tiny sign that I saw to my left when I was walking in the hospital door that read, "No children allowed." But within a few hours of running up the steps to be with my mom and spending some time with her (the last few moments that I could), then running down the steps to the car to be with my husband and baby, I was exhausted. The baby was crying, and I was crying, and my family members in my mom's room were crying. (Everybody was crying, if you hadn't noticed that theme.) I realized that I couldn't be there for anyone, let alone myself. I really tried to play by the rules. Then, I said, "F" it. I mean, after all, I gave birth at home against all the advice of medical professionals warning me that hospitals are a safer place for babies. How bad could it be if I brought my baby into this hospital, even though this little teeny tiny plaque as you walked in said no kids were allowed?

So I brought him in. My five other children were at home—I have seven children now, at the time of writing this book—sometimes with caretakers, available family, or the eldest siblings looking out for the younger kids. It was at that moment that I asked my husband to please go home and be with the kids because they're losing their Nonna, too. I let him know that I would be upstairs with the baby and my mom. She blessedly made it through the night, so after a lot of consideration, I ran home with the baby to give him a more comfortable space to sleep for just a few hours. In the morning, I ran him back into the hospital, but not before I stopped at the coffee shop next door to grab croissants and coffee for my dad, who was losing the love of his life. As I did that, I remember thinking, *This cashier has no idea my mom is dying. These people in this coffee shop, sipping coffee, have no idea that my mom is passing away right now, right next door.* I pondered these thoughts as I juggled the cardboard cup holder containing the sloshing to-go coffees, and I crushed the croissants in the white crinkled paper bag in my other hand, which I also attempted to keep steady as I cradled the large handle from my baby boy's infant carrier.

When I finally arrived upstairs and walked past the purple paper butterflies on her door frame signifying that the patient beyond that door was dying, I plopped into a chair and divvied up the croissants and coffees among my dad and brothers. Then came that dreaded "knock, knock, knock, knock" on the closed door. My sister-in-law's soft footsteps pattered against the linoleum floor as she made her way to the door. I heard some mumbling male voices, and she turned around and looked at me sheepishly. Before she could say anything, I said, "It's me, right? I have to go." And she gently nodded in confirmation. So I hoisted my newborn baby boy up, who hadn't made a peep since we arrived and he felt like a little sack of potatoes in the carrier. With him dangling from the crook of my elbow, I walked over to my mom's bedside, holding the tears in and feeling the knot in my throat form.

"*Ciao, Mamma. Ti voglio bene.*" I whispered *Bye Mamma, I love you.* My two brothers and Dad looked at each other, dumbfounded, "What's going on? We can't let this happen. We can't let this just be like this. You need to be here. You need to be able to be here."

To which I responded, "Don't do that. Just focus on mom. This is her moment … and your moments with her. Just completely ignore the situation. I will do what I'm being asked to do, so I don't ruffle any feathers." I walked out the door of the room where *my* best friend, my mamma, was leaving me and once again walked right past the purple butterflies, symbolizing our painful reality.

As I walked briskly, deeply breathing, trying to contain my emotions, I was followed by the two security guards who had knocked on the door. The same ones who had come to let us know that I needed to leave with my baby, I scowled, and holding my breath and sucking the tears in, I walked out with my twin brother by my side, determined not to make eye contact with any curious bystanders, who even out of just the corners of my eyes, were visibly taken aback by the scene of an emotionally charged little woman carrying her baby in a baby carrier, followed closely by two security guards.

As we walked out of the hospital room and under the fluorescent lights of the hallway, down an elevator, and through the exit, everybody was staring at us. The people we passed had a perplexed look. I'm sure their gears were turning with all the possible scenarios about why a short brunette with a newborn baby, soundly sleeping in his carrier, would need to be escorted out by not one, but *two*, security guards.

At this point, my husband was at home with the rest of the kids. I put my baby in the car, and I drove home, trying to regroup and process what just happened.

At home, I kept trying to think of a solution: Was there some way I could continue to be there with my mom *and* be with my baby?

It was Easter Sunday, and I was sleep deprived and emotionally exhausted, but after a short nap with the baby, more family came over. Maybe you're wondering, *Couldn't you just have left the baby with somebody else? Isn't there somebody who could have supported you?* But if you're familiar with breastfeeding, you may understand the problem: You can try everything to get your baby to take a bottle sometimes, but if this baby just wants to breastfeed, you don't get to choose. And there's nothing more you can do. But besides all this, I *wanted* to be there with my nursing baby, *and* I wanted to be there with my mom. I do not believe that anyone should have to choose between the two because of a hospital policy designed to protect the hospital from liability. Through all of the sleep deprivation, I couldn't think of a better solution. My mind still ruminates now and then about the many ways I could have done things differently. But I trust in God, and *know* that isn't Him showing up in my head with doubt. And I know that I took the steps and made the decisions that I was meant to at that divine time.

Soon, the family members who came to my house organized an Easter egg hunt outside to bring some cheer to the kids who were losing their Nonna. Sleep deprived, dejected, and depleted—baby on breast—I couldn't bring myself to go out there and participate.

But at that moment, from inside my home, I could see the clouds part, and the sun shone as brightly as I've ever seen it. Certainly, the brightest on that day. And in that moment, I received the text message from my sister, "Mom's dead."

"Oh, no," I wailed. Those around me jumped and asked urgently, "What? What is it?"

"My mom's gone," I said in a quiet, monotone voice. I then scrambled to gather my things and got my baby ready to rush back over to the hospital, almost as if I could stop it. As if by moving quickly enough, I could do something about it.

My husband and I hopped in the car with our baby and rode in silence. After a few minutes, I felt sobs surge through me that escalated into wails. "I'm sorry, Marta," my husband whispered.

When we arrived, my husband stayed in the car with our baby. I ran upstairs to meet my family. I said goodbye one last time to my mom, who at this point was already gone. And almost as if nothing devastating just happened, we all just chit-chatted, exchanged memories of her, waiting for the professionals to come and retrieve her, with tears sneaking through our stories as we honored her existence with our words, celebrating her life.

In these moments, we also leaned on comedic humor and made jokes about the baby already being a rebel without a cause, getting kicked out of hospitals and taking names. We jokingly made plans for where to get him newborn-sized prison onesies.

At that time, I remember thinking that the situation was so comically, horribly bad that there had to be some reason behind it. And it's in that moment that I went down the infamous rabbit hole that led me to my destined path.

I began learning about life insurance and digging deeper into end-of-life care, studying retirement accounts, and researching what could have been done differently.

Of course, everything happens as it should. Everything unfolds as it's meant to, but I always ask, *What can you take from the situation? What can you learn from it? How is this happening for you?* And that's how I became so engrossed in understanding how to prepare for retirement, and how life insurance policies work, including the accelerated death benefit rider. (And if you don't know if you have that or if your life insurance has it, you need to talk to me so we can look into it because that is the sole reason I became licensed to sell life insurance.)

And then, subsequently, I became licensed to sell securities, which means selling investment tools such as Roth IRAs, IRAs, simple IRAs, 529 plans, and similar investment products.

When I was growing up, my mom had made me promise that I would always take care of her. She did not want to pass in a skilled nursing facility or in a hospital, but in the end, she chose the hospital because she felt that was where she would get the best care for herself and her family. But I want you to have the end-of-life care that you would want to a T, one hundred percent.

God always provides in His most miraculous ways. But He also equips you with the knowledge to make the best decisions that you can for the best life, beginning to end.

As I became more and more engrossed in this industry, I also had a marketing agency to run that I had started over a decade prior. It was all about social media, marketing, and email strategies: open rates, insights, and algorithms. But when my best friend, my mamma, my partner in crime, left this earth, it all started to feel meaningless. And as that feeling set in, energetically, my marketing agency shifted big time.

Grief does that. My mom was my sounding board any time there was a big change in our lives, like what schools we should send the kids to. She was always there to offer her feedback. We welcomed it. If she came over and saw that the fridge was empty, she would surprise you with what she knew you needed without you telling her. If a holiday or a child's special event was coming up that required the kids' clothing to have a certain pizzazz, she arrived with bags upon bags of outfit choices. She was the kind of person who anticipated your needs and met them before you could even think about it, because she had had five children and understood what it was like to be a working mom with many children. She wanted to be there for you.

My person died and I didn't get to be with her. So, in that moment, I decided to turn my grief into growth by asking: What can I take from this situation?

I started thinking nothing else matters but life and quality of life. Honestly and truly, who gives an "F" how many clicks are happening on this ad? Who gives an "F" about conversion rates of the marketing efforts? So I dug deeper in my marketing agency as well, vowing to only serve positive-hearted clients who truly made others' lives better. And obviously, I continued to serve my clients the best that I could, going above and beyond in ways that felt aligned to fully care for the clients who trusted me with their brands. I shifted the focus to be more meaningful to me. I shifted from doing marketing for anyone and everyone to helping holistic practitioners and beauty brands. Specifically, those who allow others to live their best lives and fend off diseases with beauty and wellness solutions that allow you to feel like your best self and infuse more life into the years that you have on this earth.

And that felt more fulfilling, but it still didn't divinely click one hundred percent.

Simultaneously, my husband was experiencing difficulties with his land development endeavors that were beyond his control, so it was a very difficult time. It became a tough time financially, and I honestly just kept doing what I could. It feels to me now like I just kept throwing money at problems to fix them, and in doing so, it just exacerbated issues. But when you're deep in grief—as much as my daily life was all about thriving and living my best life, trusting the divine economy, and preaching it more than ever before—that "best life" started to feel disconnected.

The grief took me down a path of near self-sabotage, where I stopped doing my daily practices of journaling, meditating, exercising, positive thinking, and infusing myself with divine truths daily. I started to believe circumstantial facts, human facts, over the divine truth of wealth consciousness. And that energetically spiraled me further down.

When I realized I was in this downward spiral, I decided I would show up as my whole self and be fully present for my clients, committing to both parties having the best time and bringing our highest elements forward. I committed to being there for them, to witness their careers, and I felt deeply into how special and how honored I was to be there for them. I did my absolute best to be my highest version of myself for them, in alignment with the divine truth and in alignment with the way that it lit me and them up.

And as these energetics and mindsets shifted, God rewarded both my clients and me exponentially, but something was still missing. I kept running my marketing agency, while at the same time educating myself in the financial rep and life insurance rep fields because it felt like I should be doing both. I felt like, well, as long as the marketing agency is making good money, I should keep doing it. I'm good at it. It's fun. But something just didn't feel fully in alignment. I'm not surprised that, slowly but surely, even clients that I had for years, who I loved, and whose work in this world is so important and lit me up so much, were having conversations with me about being unclear of their future path. Many expressed that they wanted to pause the marketing services indefinitely. As contracts ended, they weren't being renewed, and I didn't have the aligned energy to keep seeking new ones.

In addition, if you're familiar with the United States economy from 2022 to 2025, we were experiencing what I like to call "the human economy." What I mean by that is, despite my deep trust in God's divine economy, as humans we go through economic cycles, and as a nation we were in contraction. Gas prices were skyrocketing, food prices were inflating, and the world was concerned. Because of this, instead of consumers prioritizing the services that my clients provided, which are very often out-of-pocket expenses, people were choosing routes for their health and wellness that were covered by insurance or choosing simply to go without them. People were concerned about their bottom lines and budgets, which left my otherwise successful clients without a marketing budget.

I took this as another sign. God was clearly directing me to focus on this path of becoming a financial rep for families and help them prepare for circumstances like I had just been through myself, utilizing my experience to help my clients make more confident financial decisions in their daily lives not based on fear but on an alignment of what they want for their lives.

I am so grateful every day that I get to be a financial rep and a life insurance rep to so many families, helping them find hidden money in their lives. I love teaching clients how to potentially grow their money and how to avoid a lot of the mistakes that I've made, so they can make more confident financial decisions for their divine path., I want to help my clients live the best life that they can. I also still get to have that marketing aspect by running my top-ranking podcast, my independent content creation, and spokesperson services. When I got to focus on what was lighting me up more, it became very clear that that's where God wanted me.

I decided in 2024 to close MEDIA - The Creative Agency, and I started a new entity, Whole Truth Communications LLC, through which I only do the kind of marketing that lights me up. I get to provide content creation, marketing consulting and spokesperson services to lifestyle, family, health and wellness, and beauty brands, and I get to do that as an individual. I get to have so much fun doing that through my Instagram and other social media platforms because I energetically closed the doors on what was no longer in alignment and opened new doors. God has certainly rewarded me and our family accordingly. In the meantime, my big brother decided to take the offered severance package from his federal job and focus on his zone of genius through his Emmy-award-winning videography and photography company, where I get to partner with him in business and project development. Now, we both operate in our zones of genius together.

Through my financial rep company, I get to help so many families learn if they're on track for retirement, what kind of life insurance they have, and how to make confident monetary decisions. For so long, I was making fear-based choices that were not informed, and I kept throwing money at experts to help me when it just kept spiraling because I wasn't doing the things that I teach families to do now.

I often have calls with families where they'll say, "Marta, you helped me so much. I feel so much more relaxed about our finances." They're crying tears of joy because we have solutions, and sometimes, we find wins that they hadn't even thought about. I get rewarded significantly by seeing their reactions when they have a full plan right in front of them. Sometimes, just looking at everything with somebody alongside you who is judgment-free and full of love for you and your family significantly raises your wealth consciousness so many levels of high vibrations. In other words, you feel like you have a solid financial plan that puts you at ease, which is the best state to be in for moving forward.

And I get to do that! God brought me to this divine work through the painful journey of losing my mom right after my son was born. And mind you, my mom was a hustler when it came to me and supporting me and my siblings in our professional endeavors, even from her many hospital beds. For example, during periods when I was a family photographer, if she saw a nurse who was pregnant, she would say, "Oh, my daughter is a photographer. Let me give you her card. You should contact her for newborn photos." I'm sure the nurses were like, "OK, honey." Or she would see somebody with an engagement ring as she'd be going through chemo, and she would say, "Oh, are you engaged? Do you have a photographer? My daughter and my son are wedding photographers." She was our biggest supporter. She would always proclaim, "Make the most of the opportunities and the moments that are presented to you." So it makes sense she would be all about *our* experience with her passing, leading me to my new passion.

And also, I promised her I would.

Two days before her passing, she asked me, "Will you miss me?" And normally, I would wave her off and say, "OK, come on, mom. We're not having these conversations."

But I felt like this time was different. And so when she said, "Will you miss me?" I said, "Mom, of course I'm gonna miss you so much." And she said, "But will you always miss me?" And I said, "Mom, I will *always* miss you." And I can tell you that three years later, as I write this, I still miss her. It still gets sentimental around her birthday and the anniversary of her passing. But this is my way of missing her and making the most of her life and her existence, carrying her name forward through everything that I do professionally. My mom was the biggest helper. She was known for her volunteer work. She was known for her decades of inspiring students through her teaching, from elementary school to university.

Her students loved her. And she was never judgmental about people's situations. She was the first to offer help, even when she could use help herself. She was the most selfless, kind woman who would drop everything to be there for her family. And this is the best way that I can think of to carry on her name and her legacy: by helping other families. She was brutally honest and feisty when she needed to be, and I get those qualities from her, too. She would never BS you, and I won't either.

The what-ifs still impale me. They hit me out of the blue in the quiet moments. What if we'd brought her to her home instead of the hospital to be fully present by her bedside? What if I'd insisted that she come stay with us those last few weeks? That's what I'd always promised her. But I know those thoughts aren't helpful, and they don't come from a place of self-love or love for her, even. A quote reached me recently that helped, and it was something along the lines of, *You made those promises to her when you couldn't possibly know what you could promise. You made those promises during a time when she and you were completely different people.* That reminder and the knowing that everything happens as it should, when it's meant to, and as God intends, also help me understand that this experience was so horribly, tragically awful, that it was *meant* to transform me into something more—into someone who can learn from it and help people *because* of it.

So reach out to me for help if this calls to you.

I specialize in working with families that are in the beginning to mid stages of their wealth journey to ensure that they're on the path that they'd like to be financially. We ensure your money is working for you in the most productive way in ways of investing. And if you have debt, we will map out the best and quickest way that you can take care of it before it gets on top of you like it got on top of me in the past. I'll also help you make better, more confident financial decisions and ensure that you're properly insured through your life insurance so your family is fully taken care of if something happens. I see it every day, not with my clients, but in other scenarios where, within a few years, even if families had life insurance, they're starting GoFundMe pages because they didn't have enough life insurance and are on the verge of losing their house.

I don't believe in leading with fear, but I do believe in preparing through wisdom. Financial insecurity while grieving is something that can be avoided if you have proper life insurance. If you get it early enough in life, the premiums are not that much added to your monthly budget. And it can add exponential coverage. For one client who was super healthy, for example, I was able to get him a premium of less than a hundred bucks per month for a million-plus-dollar policy. So we can save you a significant amount of money to ensure that you're properly covered.

But it is so much more than these logistics for me and for you; it's about energetics, divine truth, mindset shifts, and leading in your power as a thought leader, allowing your dreams, desires, and goals to lead you rather than all of the noise around you. Let me come alongside you and help you walk that path.

When my mom started on her difficult health journey, I worried so much about feeling alone once she was gone. She was my person. But sometimes, even when the worst-case scenario happens, we end up being OK. We're safe. We evolve through it. Her own mamma, my Nonna Zesa, passed a few years after her. Before my mom, her brother passed of cancer, as well. I like to think they're all together watching over us. I still get to talk to them every day as I share moments of my life with them, praying for guidance and gifts from heaven. Miracles happen regularly that seem to have their exact spiritual signatures on them. And for all of this, I am grateful.

About Marta

Marta Sauret Greca has received multiple awards in her journey as an entrepreneur, like Woman Business Leader of the Year, Most Influential Marketing & Entrepreneurship Expert 2025 (Pennsylvania), and more. Her books, *The Minimalist Method: The Emerging Entrepreneur's Guide to Peace and Prosperity* and *Powerful Synergy,* are both number one bestsellers on Amazon. She has been featured in national media outlets like KDKA, WPXI, the TODAY show blog, and *Inspiring Lives Magazine.*

With over ten years of marketing experience, Marta also serves as a spokesperson, content creator, speaker, and consultant for countless holistic and family brands.

Through her financial rep business, Marta helps families protect their financial peace by planning for the future and easing the stigma of societal financial burdens.

She is a mom of seven who loves spending time with her kids, their Doodle, and chickens, and being in the great outdoors.

As someone who emigrated from Italy at nine years old, Marta is fluent in both Italian and French, and is a citizen of both Italy and France.

Marta finds inspiration through her father, her late mother, and her extended and ancestral family.

She is always game to be a contributing expert on upcoming shows internationally or a speaker at your upcoming event.

Connect with Marta through her Instagram at https://www.instagram.com/martasauretgreca/

Living Gently

Jennie Askins

It was Tuesday, May 16, 2023, when my life changed forever. I heard the words we all dread, "You have cancer," told to my father while in the hospital emergency room. My whole body shook, and I felt a rush of heat take over. One part of me was paralyzed, frozen in time, the other part wanted to run, pretending I didn't hear what I heard. On some level, I knew my dad wasn't well—call it intuition—and I'm sure a part of him knew that as well, but our fear of how the bad news would change our lives kept us from facing the inevitable.

Once my dad heard the news, I could see the look of fear mixed with denial on his face. I set my emotions aside and told him we would do whatever we could as a family to help him. I told him, "Know you're not alone," but inside, I was dying. That scared little girl in me was not ready to lose her dad, but seeing the doctor's face, I knew it wasn't good. I knew right then he wasn't going to be with us for much longer.

He spent the week of the sixteenth in the hospital. One morning, when I went to his room, he told me he had a dream that he was on a white staircase. He said he was at the bottom of the staircase, and the patient in the next room was somewhere in the middle of the staircase. Then he told me he couldn't see where it was leading. As a meditation teacher with a strong faith in God and the afterlife, I knew what this meant: his time here on earth was slowly coming to an end, and he was climbing the staircase back to our creator.

I watched my dad battle this disease for almost a year. It was hard on my whole family to watch this strong man wither away. He passed on June 9, 2024. I'm so grateful we were able to spend one more year with him. My dad was a wise and brilliant man—one of the smartest men I've ever known. He had taught me so much about life. My dad also instilled a lot of wisdom in my two daughters. I am so grateful they had the privilege of knowing their papa. I have always had a strong faith in God. I believe there is a higher power and perfect order to life. I want to share the wisdom my dad has taught me and how I'm dealing with the grief from his passing. I am also sharing my views about the afterlife, not just from the standpoint of losing my dad, but also from the standpoint of being a meditation teacher and working with many different clients.

Some people hear "the afterlife" and think of it as taboo, but truth be told, there is a very thin veil between this life and what comes next. If we pay attention, we get signs all of the time from our loved ones in heaven, but you must open your heart wide enough to see the signs. The well-known saying, "ask and you shall receive," also applies when you are trying to communicate with a loved one who has passed on. Ask for a sign, have faith, have an open heart, and when you see the sign, you'll know it's from the heavens above. My dad, for example, sends me a lot of signs through deer. When he was alive, he used to feed deer in his yard. So, now when I pray or ask him to send me a sign, I usually see a deer, or the sky looks so inviting to me that I know it's him saying hello.

When my dad first passed—the very first week—I would go to bed scared at night, my nervous system was in high gear. My body was still holding on to a lot of trauma from watching him sick and withering away before my very eyes, not to mention, he was a stable force in my life who was now gone. Life as I once knew it would never be the same. I knew I had to rebuild my life. My kids needed me, and I have a strong sense of purpose in this life, so I knew I needed to go on. I wasn't a stranger to hurt, having been through a painful divorce. I knew that feeling of heaviness all too well, but I also knew that, with time, the pain eases up. I would lie in bed at night and do my deep breathing, feeling the pain. I know from experience and my training on emotional regulation that when we run from the pain inside, it persists. I breathe into it, I feel the pain, and I let it go through my body. At times, I would feel paralyzed by the pain, but I wouldn't fight it. I would pray, breathe, and meditate. I would put on headphones and do a guided meditation or listen to beautiful healing music and let the emotions flow through me, however they needed to.

First Month

The first month after my dad's death was a blur. My body and mind were still in shock. My parents were still together when my dad passed, so when I would go to my parents' home to see my mom, I felt very uncomfortable there. I felt like something was missing. At times, I thought I could see my dad working in his yard like he once did, but it wasn't comforting for me; it was a sheer pain because the reality was he wasn't there—he was gone.

Every time I went over to their house, I was hit with the reality that my dad wasn't there. I remember sitting by my parents' pool watching my brother put chemicals in the pool, and I lost it. I started crying because it brought back the memory of my dad by the pool, chatting while he put the chemicals in. It was as if someone was stabbing my heart because he was gone, and I would never witness him doing that again.

The first month was hard. I didn't feel like myself at all. I felt tired and drained. This was the time I started questioning where we go when this life is over. I was raised catholic. I knew God existed, but I still had questions: *Will I see my dad again? Can my dad still see me? Can my dad hear me if I go to talk with him?* I felt angry at this point. I started asking God why he took him, and I allowed myself the grace of asking these questions and feeling what I was feeling. The beauty of all of this was that I wasn't judging myself for asking these questions. I don't always believe in blind faith. It's healthy to explore our thoughts and feelings with these powerful questions and listen for answers. I've always considered myself somewhat of a seeker. I truly believe that because I wasn't judging the questions or feelings that were coming up for me, the answers were starting to come in. If I needed to cry, I would cry. If I felt like lying on my couch and resting, that's exactly what I did with zero judgment. This is how we allow our mind and body to heal.

Three Months

Around this time, I started to be more social again. I knew my dad would have wanted me to be happy. Our loved ones who leave this world want us to be happy, not to feel guilt or pain, but to live life. One of the things my dad had said repeatedly after he was diagnosed with cancer was that he wished he hadn't rushed through life and his day-to-day tasks. My father was a successful entrepreneur, so he was very busy. But he said if he could do it over, he would slow down and not feel like he had to get everything done at once. Around this time, I started reflecting on my own life and how I rush around, cramming everything into a day. Yes, I get to check boxes, but I'm not really living; I'm not enjoying my life or being present.

I started to make a conscious effort to slow down and be more present. I got back on a plane and took my kids on a vacation after my dad died. I hadn't flown for over fifteen years because of anxiety, but I already took two plane trips in 2024, and I'm planning a third trip.

I also journaled a lot about different signs I felt I was getting from my dad. Journaling is very healing for me. Every morning, I wake up and write two to three pages in my journal. I don't judge what I'm writing, I just let the words flow out of me and onto the paper. When I finish journaling, I feel so much lighter, as if I created space in my heart for more hope. Journaling helps the heart expand. Sometimes the tears of grief would come out of nowhere. I could be doing the dishes or yoga or watching a movie, and my heart would ache. The tears would come, but that was part of the grieving process, especially early on. We grieve because we love, and instead of judging, I let the tears flow. Then, I would suddenly realize I felt lighter because I didn't hold back the tears. If we want to heal, we must feel.

Six Months

The six-month mark felt tough because I experienced my first holiday without my dad. It was starting to sink in that I would never see my dad again while I'm on this earth—not in the way I once knew him. When I thought of him around this time, I felt like I was hitting up against a wall. It's like my heart was blocked, saddened. It felt so final. It felt like life was harder without him. I would recall him being sick, and my body would tense up from still holding on to the trauma. I cried so hard one day when I went to visit him at the cemetery that I couldn't catch my breath.

I was worried about my mom as well: how she was dealing with her grief and how much her life had changed. That is when it hit me: I had to quit trying to control everything in my life. It was time to Surrender—yes, with a capital "s." Surrender to the greater plan. You would think I would know this as a meditation teacher, but I'm human and have real struggles like anyone else. That is when I gave it truly over to God through prayer, meditation, and my writings. Shortly after, I came across a book that really spoke to me: *Talking to Heaven: A Medium's Message of Life After Death* by James Van Praagh. This book has helped me feel more connected to God, my dad, and other loved ones who have passed on. My prayers were answered—this beautiful book brought me clarity, and I started getting clients who also had lost a loved one and told me stories about how their loved ones saw relatives who passed on while they were passing. Then, a therapist friend told me a story of her near-death experience and how she felt elated, peaceful, and a sense of love she had never felt before in her life when it happened. She said she did not want to come back. After hearing these stories, I felt a sense of comfort and peace, knowing my dad was OK, and I opened up more to others about my emotions and feelings. If you experience loss, find people you feel safe chatting with. I believe we are all here to help one another grow, heal, and love.

Present Time

It has been almost a year since my dad left this world. I miss him every single day. I know I will grieve forever, but the heaviness is gone. I'm grateful for the footprints he left on my heart and the hearts of my daughters. Since his death, I'm slowing down, I'm surrendering, I'm enjoying the little things … and most of all, I'm keeping my heart open for those little signs from him.

If you're grieving, invite in moments when you feel pure joy, moments where you feel like you're experiencing heaven right here on earth. To see and feel these moments, we must be present and have an open heart. Appreciate those in your life, for moments together are fleeting. We think someone is going to be here with us forever until, *poof*, they're gone. I'm living gently with others, gently with myself, and gently with life, for life is precious.

At the end of one's life, people often express regrets about not living a life true to themselves. Go live your life, wake up every day, and think of at least three things to be grateful for, listen to your intuition, and surrender to each moment. Then, watch the miracles unfold before you.

I want to leave you with a couple of notable James Askins's lines to inspire your journey.

"There is a perfect timing for everything."

"When the apple is ripe, it will fall."

"Eagles don't follow the flock; be an eagle."

About Jennie

Jennie Askins is an entrepreneur and the creator of the Mind-Body-Shift (MBS) Method, as well as the host of the Unapologetically U podcast.

Jennie's specialty is to help *you* create positive and lasting change. She teaches people how to reach for a better version of themselves. Jennie does this through her MBS Method, in which she incorporates movement, meditation, mindfulness, yoga, breathwork, and somatic therapy to help you heal mentally, physically, and spiritually. Jennie has dedicated her practice to helping others heal.

Jennie published *Connecting Within* in 2019, a self-help book to help new moms on their journey to balance, peace, and joy. At the end of each chapter is a meditation and journaling prompt to help moms rediscover their inner peace.

Jennie's degree and background is in business management and marketing, but in 2018, she needed a change so she became certified in meditation and mindfulness practices, in 2020 she became a certified life and spiritual coach from Life Purpose Institute based out of San Diego, Ca., and in 2022 a Hatha yoga instructor through Yoga Alliance. She feels she is on her true, authentic path and living her purpose. That is why Jennie finds such great joy in helping others find their true purpose and path.

Connect with Jennie
jennieaskins@gmail.com
https://mindbodyandshift.com/
https://youtube.com/@unapologeticallyu11
https://unapologeticallyu.buzzsprout.com/

Lifequakes and the Calling They Unleash

Heather Cherry

Bruce Feiler, author of *Life Is in the Transitions: Mastering Change at Any Age*, says we experience three to five "lifequakes" in our lives—major upheavals that can last up to five years.[1] That means nearly half of our adult lives are spent in transition. If you're not going through one now, someone close to you probably is.

A lifequake isn't just a setback—it's an aftershock moment that alters everything. Think: death, disease, job loss, a new baby, a move, a crisis. And for me, those moments didn't come one at a time. For a while, they came simultaneously and with an unrelenting ferocity.

The first hit when I was just twenty-two. I lost my first full-time job in 2009—right in the middle of the recession. It was devastating but oddly hopeful. I was still in college, on track to graduate with an interior design degree. I believed my creative career was waiting just around the corner.

What I didn't realize then was how hard it would be to break into a creative field in rural Pennsylvania during an economic downturn. Still, I kept aiming, applying, and hoping for a colorful, inspired future.

Then I got married. And then I got pregnant.

Still without a creative career, I started freelance writing. It wasn't the plan, but it gave me a sense of control and alignment. I couldn't find the job I wanted, so I built one. For three years, life felt steady.

Until it didn't.

---

[1]https://www.brucefeiler.com/books-articles/life-is-in-the-transitions/

Another lifequake came: my husband was injured, and shortly after, we found out we were expecting again. It felt serendipitous—like life had its own plan. My freelance work wasn't thriving, but I felt fulfilled and grounded by this new chapter.

And then came November 15, 2013.

Our second son arrived slightly early, similar to our first. We were overjoyed and soaking in the newborn bliss. But just nine days later, I had to say goodbye. He had an underdeveloped lung, requiring ECMO support (a life support therapy that takes over the function of the lungs and heart when they are severely impaired). Eventually, his body gave out from multi-organ failure.

There are no words for the ache. I was shattered. I still had a toddler who needed me, but my heart grieved the child I barely got to know. I was filled with despair, guilt, and deep regret. We hadn't known anything was wrong during the pregnancy. I had even opted for a tubal ligation during delivery, before we uncovered the severity of his condition.

Oddly enough, this wasn't yet my rock bottom.

Despite the darkness, a part of me still believed this pain had to mean something. I clung to the idea that I was meant for more—even if I couldn't see what that was yet.

In the year that followed, we moved. We sold everything and started over in a new town. The new beginning offered a fresh start, but soon we experienced more loss: family deaths, more job changes. My career continued to meander through roles I didn't love, while freelance writing remained a side gig, lingering in the background.

Self-employment always called to me. The freedom, the creative control, the alignment with my values—it all made sense. But in a world that idolizes security and full-time W-2 jobs, it felt like a risky fantasy.

Still, I kept going. I knew I had already lost too much to settle for a life that didn't feel like mine. I wanted a career that allowed me to *live*—to raise my son with presence, to choose joy, to build something meaningful.

Then came 2019 … and the most toxic workplace I'd ever experienced.

I was thrilled to land a new job that seemed to offer everything I'd been waiting for: creativity, autonomy, and a chance to grow. But the red flags emerged immediately. I wasn't provided the tools I needed—no laptop, no support, no guidance—and was ridiculed for trying to solve problems on my own.

I remember one moment vividly. I had created a brochure—a task I had done countless times. The executive director said nothing, disappeared, then returned with her own version. "This is what I wanted. Just like this," she snapped, slamming it on my desk.

Her micromanagement chipped away at my confidence. I was demeaned for asking questions. Dismissed for needing flexibility that had been promised. It culminated when I came to work, got sick, and was reprimanded for asking to leave.

The final straw? Timing my bathroom breaks.

That was it. Something in me broke—but in a good way. I realized: *I deserve better. I have lived through more than most people know. I am too grown, too capable, and too called to be treated like a child.*

I didn't wait. I quit on the spot—no notice, no safety net. It was the boldest move I'd ever made.

And it changed everything.

I went all in on my freelance writing business. I had no idea how I'd replace my paycheck, but I knew I would never go back to that kind of life again. I marketed, pitched, networked, and put into practice everything I had learned over the years. Each morning, I woke up excited. For the first time, I felt aligned with my purpose.

Then, the pandemic hit.

Almost overnight, the client list I had built evaporated. Fear crept in where clarity had once been. I was back at square one.

But I didn't give up. I regrouped. I reimagined. I started over … again. Because resilience had become part of who I am.

Later that year, I accepted another full-time job, which felt like a dream opportunity. It worked for a while. Until it didn't. In January 2024, I was laid off. Once again, I was forced into full-time freelance.

Only this time, I was ready for it.

Through it all—grief, upheaval, toxic bosses, relocations, and reinventions—I've come to believe this: *we don't need to define ourselves so rigidly.* As women, especially, we box ourselves in—feeling like we must choose between motherhood or ambition, stability or freedom, healing or hustle.

But the truth is, the magic lives in the *intersection.*

We are allowed to evolve. We are allowed to redefine. We are allowed to walk away and start again. Not because we failed, but because we're finally listening to that divine nudge guiding us back to ourselves.

Gone are the days of letting others control my destiny.

I've also come to realize that maybe my true calling isn't a single job or title—it's a way of living. A way of showing up honestly, fully, and in service of others who are navigating their own uncertain paths. What I once saw as detours, I now recognize as divine direction.

For years, I thought that if I could just figure out my career, everything else would fall into place. But the truth is, it was in the unraveling that I discovered what truly mattered. I learned to live in the intersections—where motherhood meets ambition, where grief meets growth, and where purpose doesn't demand perfection, only presence.

But learning to live this way didn't come naturally—it came out of necessity.

I didn't grow up with a clear sense of who I was. It wasn't because I lacked love or safety. My parents were doing the best they could with the struggles life had handed them, but they were often too consumed with surviving their own storms to help me name or nurture my identity. So, like many kids, I learned to adapt. I did what I had to do to get by. I jumped in headfirst and figured it out as I went.

That pattern—improvising, adjusting, trying, and failing—followed me into adulthood. Some saw it as reckless. Others assumed I was "half-assing" my way through life. But the truth is, this is how I learn. I try. I get it wrong. I try again. And honestly, that's a vital trait for entrepreneurs—even if the world doesn't always value it.

We live in a culture obsessed with definition and proof. We're taught to label ourselves neatly and show the receipts to back it up. But how can we define who we are without ever making mistakes? How can we know if we like or hate something if we've never given ourselves the freedom to try it? Maybe we didn't like broccoli the first time because it was steamed, but once it's roasted with garlic and olive oil, it's delicious.

We give up too easily. We shame ourselves for detours. But what if the detour *is* the direction?

I've heard the phrase "everything happens for a reason" more times than I can count. And while I understand the intent, I can't accept that every tragedy is divinely calculated. I can't tell a grieving mother—myself included—that losing a child happened *for* a reason. That's not comforting. That's crushing.

So I've reframed it.

To me, failure isn't a verdict—it's a redirection. It's a signpost. A whisper from God, the universe, or your soul that says: *Not this way. Try again. Keep going.*

I've tattooed that reminder on my arm: *Failure is redirection.*

Because when I'm stuck, scared, or starting over, I need to see it. I need to believe that what looks like the end might actually be the beginning of something better. A different route. A wiser approach. A fresh take, like roasting the broccoli instead of steaming it.

You don't need to reinvent everything. Sometimes the shift is subtle but sacred. A small change. A new rhythm. A fresh boundary. One honest "no" that makes room for a much more aligned "yes."

And that's where I am now.

No longer rushing to define myself for the sake of others. No longer apologizing for not fitting into the mold. I'm showing up with the fullness of my experience—grief, grit, growth—and offering it in service of something greater.

Because this isn't just about a career anymore.

It's about raising my son in ways I never got to be raised. It's about building a business that feels like home. It's about trusting the quiet divine nudges, even when the path isn't clear. And most of all, it's about helping others listen to that same inner voice—the one that's been whispering all along:

You are not lost. You are being realigned. You are not behind. You are becoming.

So if you're standing at the edge of a lifequake—if the ground beneath you feels unsteady or unfamiliar—take heart. You are not broken. You are being rebuilt. Trust the redirection. Trust your resilience. And most of all, trust that even in your most uncertain moments, you are being led. Your divine path isn't waiting on perfection; it's waiting on your *yes*. One small yes at a time. One brave, imperfect, wholehearted step forward. You're not starting over—you're starting again, but this time, from experience.

About Heather

Heather Cherry is a health and wellness writer, certified health coach, and lifelong storyteller. She specializes in creating content that bridges the gap between science and everyday life, making complex topics accessible, actionable, and human. Her work has appeared in national outlets like *SELF*, *Forbes*, and *Business Insider*, and she's passionate about helping others feel seen through stories that matter. When she's not writing, Heather enjoys exploring the outdoors with her family and geeking out over functional nutrition. This is her first anthology contribution, and she's honored to share a piece of her journey.

Connect with Heather
Website: https://www.heathercherry.com
Portfolio: https://heathercherry.journoportfolio.com

Instagram:
https://www.instagram.com/heathercherry.writer.coach
LinkedIn: https://www.linkedin.com/in/heather-cherry

From Semi-Retired to RE-FIRED!

Dorothy L. Clear

There are two things you should know about me. The first is that I have led a very active lifestyle since I was a young girl. Sports, athletics, and competition are as natural to me as a fish breathing underwater. I was on roller skates since I could walk. My knees were always scabbed up. I went swimming at the neighborhood pool daily during the summer, took swimming lessons, and participated in competitive diving.

In elementary school, I played basketball. In high school, I continued playing basketball, played flag football, and was on the drill team, which marched in local parades. After I finished school, I started playing in neighborhood softball leagues and got involved in coed volleyball and bocce. Racquetball became my obsession in college, and I worked part-time at a fitness center teaching a beginner's exercise class.

I played wallyball at the YMCA three days a week and was still playing in 2018. (Wallyball is volleyball played on a racquetball court, so the ball can bounce off the walls and ceiling during a volley.) I do not know when I stopped playing, but I remember it was getting harder and harder to recover. I would come home after two hours on the court, and my hands and feet hurt so badly that I would run my hands under icy water in the kitchen sink to ease the pain. Following the example of other players, I began wearing sports gloves to reduce the pain. After two hours of wallyball, I usually needed a nap.

Hiking was also becoming unbearable. By the end of the hike, I felt like knives were stabbing me between the bones in my feet. I discovered soft rubber recovery slides to slip on after taking off my tennis shoes. I would soak my feet in warm Epsom salt baths for relief.

The second thing you should know about me is that when I was *called* to be a professional organizer, I discovered my God-given talent. My soul blossomed like a flower bud opening its petals for the first time. It's the longest job I have held, *and I loved it*! Helping people to organize their homes or businesses often had a significant impact on their lives, which made me love doing it even more. I even became a Certified Professional Organizer®.

The work involved frequent bending, lifting, carrying, packing, and moving items, including furniture and other objects—all things I could do without thinking about it when I started at fifty years old. I still felt fit and strong. But in 2018, I was fifty-seven and felt I was starting to slow down, experiencing mild osteoarthritis pain in my left hip (causing bursitis) and in my left thumb, even when walking—not running—up and down steps.

At a spiritual conference with my husband that year, I explained to someone why I had so many bandages on my fingers. My skin was blistering and slow to heal. Dealing with this condition was annoying and a little embarrassing.

I was frustrated because nothing seemed to help. Carrying Band-Aids and first aid cream with me was standard. I realized I had been dealing with the problem long enough. It was time to talk to my doctor.

During my doctor's appointment in late 2018, I told her my symptoms. She asked if I had any stiffness, fatigue, or brain fog. I said, "Yes, I do have days when it's harder to concentrate. I am stiff when I get up from a seated position or get out of the car."

She prescribed a steroid ointment for my hands twice a day—once in the morning and once at bedtime—and to wear white gloves while sleeping. She referred me to a rheumatologist and a dermatologist. She suspected rheumatoid arthritis (RA) and contact dermatitis.

In January 2019, I saw a dermatologist one day and a rheumatologist the next day. The dermatologist diagnosed me with contact dermatitis. She advised me to keep using the steroid ointment, suggested an allergy panel test, prescribed a low dose of methotrexate, and told me to wear gloves for working and cleaning.

The next day, I saw the rheumatologist. She ordered blood work, which confirmed her diagnosis of RA. She recommended methotrexate, and I said, "My dermatologist prescribed that yesterday." The rheumatologist wanted to start me on biologic medication to prevent bone damage. This is given intravenously every six to eight weeks and is referred to as an infusion.

OK. Wow. That was a ton of information to process in two days! Instead of being relieved that I had answers, I was shocked and scared. I did not want to believe it (denial) and wondered how my life would change (grief). How long can I keep working? Will treatment help? How fast does it progress? I had so many questions (fear).

It is during these challenges in life that my faith saves me from all forms of anxiety, worry, depression, and fear. Helping others also keeps me grounded, humble, and out of self-pity. I learned in my mid-thirties that faith and fear cannot coexist. To the extent that I allow fear in my faith diminishes. Worrying is different from problem-solving. It is human nature to feel sorry for yourself at first. That is OK for a brief time, but then you must start living in the solution instead of the problem.

Arthritis runs on my dad's side of the family. He and his siblings had it, and my siblings have it also. I knew I had osteoarthritis (OA) and accepted that as a part of aging, but now it was time to research RA. So, I started reading everything about treatments, medications, alternative diets, and exercise. I joined Facebook groups about anti-inflammatory diet recipes, RA, and autoimmune disorders. I learned more about the differences from the Mayo Clinic, "Rheumatoid arthritis differs from the more common osteoarthritis. Some people have both. Osteoarthritis causes damage to joints from overuse. Rheumatoid arthritis affects the lining of the joints and eats away at the bone under them. This causes a painful swelling that can cause joints to bend out of shape over time, called deformity."[2]

The doctor informed me that Methotrexate causes a folate deficiency, so I was prescribed folic acid to counteract this side effect. Later, the doctor added B12 and vitamin D supplements to my treatment plan because I was deficient in these as well.

That autumn, I learned I had to stop my RA medications to get my flu shot. OK, it was inconvenient, but doable with the right scheduling. Later, I found out that I had to come off my medications anytime I got an infection, needed vaccines, or had surgery, which meant having an RA flare.

The next year, the COVID-19 pandemic hit and shut down *everything*! My work as a certified professional organizer came to an abrupt halt in March 2020. I did not have even one client for an entire month, then work started to slowly trickle in. I had to pivot my business, Clear Organization, which I had been building since 2011, or I would lose it. This was my passion in life, and I could not let it slip away. By this time, I was also a published author and paid speaker.

Because work was slow, and I had the stimulus check from the government, I seized the opportunity to enroll in the Coach Approach Training Institute in April 2020. I had been dreaming of this for years, but I could never afford the tuition. In the fall of 2021, I earned my certified neurodiversity coach (CNC) credential.

Between June and July 2020, I completed the Delson Virtual Organizing Training Program for Professional Organizers® over six weeks. These two programs enabled me to offer additional services in virtual organizing and coaching to my clients. I also thought, if I become too old to work as an organizer, I can switch to coaching.

Now, let me quickly walk you through my health struggles over the last four years and why pivoting during the pandemic was a godsend for a second time.

---

[2] https://www.mayoclinic.org/diseases-conditions/rheumatoid-arthritis/symptoms-causes/syc-20353648#dialogId51279188

<u>December 2021</u>—Rotator cuff repair surgery on my left shoulder

<u>April 2022</u>—An emergency room visit for uveitis in my right eye due to my RA. Uveitis is inflammation in the middle layer of the eye, and left untreated for a day, it is extremely painful![3]

<u>May 2022</u>—Early in the month, I got COVID. Later that month, my left knee swelled up for no apparent reason, and I could barely walk. I used a crutch for two days. I saw my PCP, had x-rays done, and was told to take NSAIDs and rest. The diagnosis was a left ACL sprain and degenerative joint disease.

<u>June and July 2022</u>—My RA treatment stopped working. This is one of the baffling problems with RA. Sometimes medicines stop working. I was experiencing extreme brain fog and exhaustion. I was getting very stiff about a week or two before my scheduled infusion. My rheumatologist prescribed hydroxychloroquine. This medication puts me at risk for retinopathy. I will need to see an ophthalmologist annually for my lifetime. She also changed my infusion medication. This was a physical nightmare!

<u>October 2022</u>—Anytime I would trip or catch my foot on something or twist it a certain way, I would get this electric shock in the back of my left knee. The pain was excruciating but temporary. I saw an orthopedist and had my knees x-rayed. He started cortisone injections.

<u>May 2023</u>—I turned sixty-two years old and decided to collect my retirement. I scaled back to working part-time as an organizer and coach. My left knee was getting more painful, but wearing a knee brace helped. By the end of summer, my right knee became painful. I often wore braces on both knees. By August, I was ready to schedule my left total knee replacement surgery. I discontinued the cortisone shots in my right knee because they were not working, and the withdrawal was even more debilitating. One weekend, I could barely walk unassisted. My husband and I went to a thrift store and bought a rollator,

---

[3] https://www.mayoclinic.org/diseases-conditions/uveitis/symptoms-causes/syc-20378734

which is a mobility aid that provides stable support and allows the user to sit comfortably.[4]

November 2023—Left total knee replacement surgery.

October 2024—I got uveitis a second time in my right eye. It was less dramatic this time because I knew what it was, and I had steroid eye drops on hand.

December 2024—Right total knee replacement surgery.

Over the last four years, I have not stopped working, but I needed to focus more on my health. I reduced my hours and considered full retirement. I stopped promoting my business, stopped networking, and rarely posted on social media. Yet clients kept coming. I gave up high-impact exercise and sports, but I still ride my motorcycle, exercise bike, or bicycle, and I walk and hike. I love to hike in state parks when I travel.

After my second knee surgery, I knew I could not meet the physical demands of organizing, but I did not want to retire. Should I shut down the business and get a part-time job or transition solely to coaching? I have worked for myself for so long, I could not imagine working for anyone else. Then, self-doubt about changing the business around would creep in. There were a myriad of decisions to make, and quite a bit of work to get it all done. Getting a job may be easier, but would I experience the same level of personal satisfaction I had come to love by working one-on-one to help people change their lives for the better?

I was going through so much mentally and physically over the two years with the knee surgeries, RA flares, and depression that I did not have the energy to change my business. These thoughts about my future would come and go. I had to trust God that I was right where I needed to be.

Then, in February 2025, a friend asked me to start coaching her to reach a goal. God works through people. The same thing happened in 2011 when a friend asked me for help organizing her home. That is how I started my coaching business.

---

[4] https://www.sciencedirect.com

Coaching my friend ignited something in me. I was still recovering from my recent knee surgery, but my passion for coaching and being an entrepreneur was ablaze! I thought I was destined to retire, but suddenly I was RE-FIRED! Life had meaning, and I was fired up. My entrepreneurial juices were flowing again.

I felt confident transitioning from organizing to coaching. By the end of March 2025, I launched my new coaching business, Clear Mindset, coaching women who identify as neurodivergent in their personal-growth journey.

I could not have continued to overcome life's trials without my relationship with a God of my understanding, a Higher Power that I rely on and trust to guide me, the Creator I express gratitude to daily and who taught me how to pray properly, a Universal Intelligence that made me, and saved me from self-destructive alcoholism twenty-nine years ago. My daily spiritual practice gives me strength and courage. My faith alleviates my fears and anxiety. I know my purpose moving forward is to help other women grow in confidence and know their strength and value. God is working through me to fulfill that purpose.

About Dorothy

After earning a bachelor's degree in business management, working more than two decades in a corporate career, thirteen years as a self-employed certified professional organizer specializing in working with grieving clients, authoring a book, *Restore Order. Restore Joy.,* appearing as an organizer on an episode of *Hoarders*, and becoming a paid conference speaker, Dorothy has accumulated a wealth of knowledge and expertise to share with her clients.

During the COVID-19 pandemic, when shutdowns made it apparent she would not be allowed to enter her professional organizing clients' homes to continue her work in person, she enrolled in two continuing education programs, earning a life coaching certification specializing in neurodiversity and support advocacy and a Certified Virtual Professional Organizer®

certificate. Adding these additional services enabled her business to survive.

In 2025, she fully transitioned from organizing to coaching with her newest business endeavor, Clear Mindset. The business offers supportive services in one-to-one or group coaching as well as workshops. The use of brain-based, evidence-backed skills helps her coaching clients find the courage and motivation to overcome adversity and move their lives forward.

Clear Mindset's mission is to empower women to foster self-esteem, learn from experience, champion positive change, be more resilient, increase self-learning, and propel their personal growth.

Connect with Dorothy
www.facebook.com/ClearMindsetCoach
https://www.instagram.com/clearmindsetcoach/
https://www.linkedin.com/in/clearmindsetcoach/

The End Result is Not the Beginning Circumstances

Lisa Fera

As a single mom working and obtaining an education, I lived in a duplex in the South Hills of Pittsburgh. I was safe and comfortable in my home, and then I received notice that I had to move. The landlord decided not to renew my lease; sadly, this was not the first time this had happened. After being told to pack and move for a second time, I decided to purchase a house so I would never be told I had to move again!

I started the adventure to find a home in my price range. It was very important to me to find a handicapped-accessible house because my brother Nicky had cerebral palsy and was in a wheelchair. The home needed to have a level entrance or a few steps. A lot of houses were eliminated based on those criteria. I then came to realize that the Cape-Cod style house directly adjacent to where I was living could be perfect. It was in my price range and had a few steps, but a portable ramp would work for Nicky to have access.

I was acquainted with the granddaughter of the man who owned the Cape Cod house, so I contacted her and learned that her grandparents would be selling the house soon. This house was the best option for us because my son could keep his neighborhood friends and school, and my brother could easily visit. I made an offer, and it was accepted.

The house had few neighbors nearby, with one next door and the one behind, which was the duplex I would be moving from. The yard was large, containing many trees. The neighborhood fostered a sense of community where people looked out for each other. Residents often sat outside talking while their children played.

My new house and life seemed perfect. I was finally able to remodel the kitchen by taking out a wall between the dining room and kitchen and installing custom hickory kitchen cabinets. As a young single mom, creating my dream kitchen was not an easy task financially, and I was proud to finally accomplish it. Soon, I was even able to start saving for retirement. All was good.

Years later, someone in the neighborhood purchased the duplex property I used to live in. Soon after, the duplex property and their residence became a dumpsite. A broken, rusted car sat in the front yard, along with wood piles, old contractor equipment, and supplies from the construction company they operated out of their home. Workers started parking in the street in front of my house, and large tractor-trailers began dropping off supplies. We were in a close-knit neighborhood ... that was falling apart. Navigating the employee cars parked on the street and coming home to the view of a dumpsite was unsettling.

To keep the peace, knowing I couldn't change the situation, I got pricing for a six-foot, L-shaped wooden fence for my yard to at least block the view of all the equipment. Sadly, the quotes weren't within my budget, but when I told my trainer at the gym, he said, "You buy the wood, and I will bring the men."

I am forever grateful for those men.

As the men were digging holes for the posts, they noticed the neighbor staring at them. They were concerned for me and my safety, living in this situation. I didn't think anything of it, though. The fence was tastefully done and attractive. I considered it a win-win: the neighbor could continue to accumulate junk, and I created peace in my space.

As some time went by, the neighbor built a four-foot cross in his side yard. It sat right at the end of the fence facing my house in the front yard. Even better, it was illuminated at night. A few weeks after the four-foot cross, he added a cross to his roof, larger than the four-foot cross in the yard. A few weeks later, I came home after watching a football game with some friends. It seemed that he was finally removing the dead pine tree from his yard, and I was relieved. The next morning I saw a forty-foot cross with lights constructed in the pine tree on his property, and it was pointing toward my house. By evening the cross was brightly lit up to the extent of lighting up the inside of my house.

I lived at the house by myself at this point, and my neighbor started harassing me. He would stand at the edge of his property and taunt me when I took my garbage out at night or stand on his second-floor unfinished deck, staring at me doing yard work. When my son was home from college, helping me in the yard, he said, "Mom, he is up there staring at us. This is creepy." That's when I realized I had to do something.

I decided to talk to the police because I felt uncomfortable, especially at night when I took my garbage out. But after talking to the police, a bigger nightmare started.

The local police chief called me to say that a reporter was on their way to my house so I could tell my story. This is when I learned how the media could spin stories to get more viewers, rather than telling the truth.

The first question the reporter asked was, "What do you think of this cross?" I said, "I don't like it." In hindsight, I should have said, "I don't like how the symbolism of Christ is being used in this situation." I was young, naïve, and scared of my neighbor's mental health.

The media blew up this story as his religious right to display the cross. I had multiple media visits that day, and by the end of the night, I said to the Channel 11 reporter, "I will only talk to you if you show the entire story. This is not about religion. Show the entire yard." The news station did, and the reporter stayed in contact with me, letting me know what he was learning. After a public council meeting, this reporter called and said how concerned he was for me and the mental health of this neighbor.

Finally, the borough was ready to issue code violations requiring him to remove the crosses. The neighbor stated the cross was pointed at me because I was the lost sheep. This had nothing to do with religion for me. It was simply about having a continuing escalation unfolding with a neighbor. I love Jesus, and Jesus is love. Those crosses did not symbolize anything Jesus stood for.

The police chief found out about a similar situation in another area that did not end well after the code violation was issued, so he informed me that the SWAT team was ready, just in case.

As weeks went by, I started thinking about selling my house, and I approached this neighbor to see if his older son might want to buy it. He raised his hand inches from my neck and said, "I can't touch you, but bring the men in your life to me, and I will work this out with them."

I slowly walked away, terrified.

Then I took matters into my own hands. I borrowed a rifle and spent some time with a marine sniper who taught me how to best defend myself with it. I learned about different types of bullets. I prepared. I did not want to own a gun, and never wanted to, but I needed to maintain my safety. I felt like something bigger was going on with my neighbor that I had no control over.

I invited the police to my house to talk about my rifle and how to legally navigate this situation. Sadly, I learned at that time, I needed to be cornered before I could shoot.

The media was still calling this a religious issue. None of them listened to me. They twisted my words to fuel the flames till it became international news—a headline in Google News. I received private messages on Facebook and phone calls full of insults.

Once my house was finally on the market, I could not even imagine who would buy it. I felt so guilty about selling to someone who did not know what was going on that I went to counseling to make sure I could help potential buyers understand the situation.

I prayed so hard. I cried. I felt alone and scared!

An offer came in from a retired teacher whose parents lived three houses away from me. She understood and knew everything, but she wanted to be close to her parents. I was relieved, but I still had to find a place to live when I sold the house. I placed everything in storage and moved in with my parents.

After several offers fell through, a house came up on the market across the street from my brother's group home. The house needed so much work! I was mentally exhausted and could not imagine how I would have the financial resources to do the work this house needed, and the house just did not feel good when I walked through it. I cried from frustration. A week later, this house was still on the market, and I was surprised because of the location. I went through the house again and decided to give it a chance. I just wanted to unpack my life from the storage unit and sleep in my own bed.

Once I moved in, I realized that I was so blessed to be across from my brother's group home. We could go for walks, and I walked across the street with my dog for visits with Nicky and the other residents in the home. My parents were relieved knowing I was just across the street from him.

I really did not want this house; God put me in this house. Being there, I appreciated the extra time I got to spend with my brother and how easy it was for him to cross the street in his electric wheelchair for visits and family gatherings.

This is when I started believing stronger in God's plan, I would never have moved from my prior home if it were not for my neighbor's accumulation of junk, building the crosses, and having what appeared to be a mental health crisis.

These events taught me that life's unpredictability can be frustrating at times, but embracing it makes the journey so much more meaningful. Every twist and turn has its purpose. There's a certain freedom in letting go of control and allowing the path to unfold as it's meant to. Keep moving forward—there's so much ahead for us to discover. Challenges are not roadblocks; they are stepping stones guiding us to where we need to be.

I learned many lessons during this journey, one of them was learning to truly turn my life circumstances over to God. The second is that the common saying "money is not everything" is not entirely accurate. Money might not solve all your problems, but it allows us choice and freedom. Your relationship with money and how you use it is important. Respect it; don't abuse it. Money alone doesn't guarantee happiness, but wise financial decisions open doors to opportunity. Even as a single mom, I was able to buy my first home and turn it into my dream home. Then I was able to find another perfect home (when the dream became a nightmare) because I had reduced overspending and saved. I was conscious of how I used my money. This puts me in a place of freedom, so I can now help others. This is why I am very passionate about being an investment advisor, helping people to achieve the life they want, when they want it, and at the exact time meant for them by God.

I am writing this in memory of my brother Nicky, who has taught us all many lessons about life! God's Power worked through my brother's life.

About Lisa

Lisa Fera's journey is an inspiring blend of service, dedication, and financial *expertise*. She began her career as an EMT/paramedic and later joined the Navy Reserves as a hospital corpsman, demonstrating a deep commitment to helping others. Her practical and compassionate nature led her to engage with medical billing at the ambulance center, ensuring essential services had the financial support to operate effectively. This experience naturally guided her toward earning an accounting degree and eventually becoming an investment advisor.

Lisa earned her degrees at the Community College of Allegheny County and Robert Morris College, strengthening her expertise in accounting and finance. She worked in tax accounting, auditing, and as a controller, where she gained firsthand knowledge of financial systems. Through these roles, she recognized the importance of investing money wisely, making financial resources work for individuals rather than just sitting idle. Earning her licenses as an investment advisor, she now applies her knowledge to helping others build financial security and stability.

Connect with Lisa
https://www.facebook.com/LisaAnnFera/
https://www.instagram.com/lisaferapfs/
https://www.linkedin.com/in/lisa-fera-5bb41a1a/
https://www.primerica.com/lisafera
www.primerica.com/lisafera

Say Yes to Distress: A Bridal Story

Jillian Forsberg

The phone, warm in my hands from so many calls, kept ringing. On my fourth try, despite the echoing death-knell sound, I was certain that someone, anyone, would answer.

My palms grew slick, and I put the phone back on its receiver. The joyful noise of a bride in the depths of the shop saying "Yes!" replaced the noise of the phone in my ears, and I clenched my jaw. I hoped, prayed, that she had not just said yes to one of our Alfred Angelo gowns.

"Kathleen, I can't reach customer service." I texted my sales rep, a woman whose fading red hair and tanned skin always reminded me of a middle-aged Ariel. But Kathleen wasn't responding, either.

Two hours earlier, the rumors hit the bridal shop I managed: the design house called Alfred Angelo was gutted, going under, done for. But the bridal designer had been around for one hundred years, and the shop I worked for had as many bridesmaids' and bridal gowns as years they'd been around. If they were done for, certainly they'd send over the completed orders we'd placed months ago ... right?

Right?! With no answer from the 1-800 customer service number and no answer from my sales rep, I started pulling paperwork.

The bridesmaid file was sorted by brides' last names, and I yanked them from their folders and sorted them.

Alfred, Alfred, Alfred. Alfred. Shit.

The shipping dates of the dresses were close, though, which meant that the designer should have completed the work and sent them. Perhaps they would arrive today! Perhaps they were in the port, and all eighty-five bridesmaid dresses we had on order would be hauled in by our UPS guy. And there would be no problems at all!

But the sickly sweet feeling in the back of my throat told me otherwise. Some of these weddings were just a month or so away.

Eighty-five bridesmaids. My stomach clenched as I pulled the bridal paperwork. How many wedding dresses ...

I sorted, keeping an eye on my cell phone and an eye on the bride, whose happy family wandered to the front desk. Whew. No Alfred Angelo gown for her.

Our newest shipment from Alfred Angelo arrived a week ago and included a staggering twenty new bridal gowns. The amount was surprising as they usually shipped two or three at a time. But our entire market order was sent in one giant box, plastered with the Alfred Angelo logo and bursting at the corners.

Glitter-covered ballgowns, fitted lacy beauties whose long trains dripped like sugar water, sleek satin with a sweetheart neckline, and my personal favorite: a corseted bohemian dress with delicate point d'esprit. The staff and I fawned over them, steamed the wrinkles out, and hung them on display.

But the owner of the shop asked me a very pointed question: "Have we ever gotten such a big box from them?"

"No," I said. "We haven't." She clutched the invoice in her hand, reading it over carefully. The shipping charge was hundreds of dollars. She shook her head lightly and tucked it into the accounts payable folder.

Now, I counted only two bridal gowns (thank God!) on order from them.

My phone buzzed with a text. Kathleen.

"Hey Jillian, give me a call."

I ducked into the small office, tucked under the stairs of the historic building where the shop had been for almost a decade, and sat, trembling.

"Kathleen? Is the news true?"

"Yeah, none of the keyholders can get into the buildings. All of the Alfred Angelo standalone shops are shuttered. I can't reach customer service either, but my boss says we're done."

I paused, straining to look at the pile of bridesmaid orders I'd left on the counter.

"So the orders will be shipped, though, if they're done?"

This time, she paused. For so long I was sure we'd been disconnected.

"Kathleen ...?"

"The bank is seizing all product to auction off and pay the debt. Alfred Angelo is bankrupt, Jillian. You won't be getting your orders."

The computer screen swirled in front of me, but I knew the monitor wasn't broken. I steadied myself. Took a deep breath.

"I've gotta go, Kathleen," I said. "Please call me if you learn anything more."

So the rumors were true. Bankrupt. Poor management. Overpromising. Unbelievable debt. A poor business model of providing gowns for small independent retailers like us and operating standalone stores meant they were in competition with themselves.

I picked up the store phone and dialed another bridal company. I needed to replace eighty-five bridesmaid dresses. And two bridal gowns.

Hours later, I had a solid plan. Of the dozen or so bridesmaid companies out there, there was a consensus: they agreed Alfred was never going to deliver, and they would pick up the orders placed with the most similar products they could at a discounted rate and expedited shipping, rushing the gowns with the closest wedding dates as quickly as they could.

I had sorted through every single gown the other companies made, flinging color swatches and comparing size charts, coming up with a plan for each bridesmaid and making sure that the brides' visions were still intact.

Now, I had to tell them their gowns were not coming. My heart fluttered as I dialed the first bride.

"Alfred Angelo has gone bankrupt, but we have a plan for you ..." I told each one of them. "I have found the most similar gowns and colors for your bridesmaids. I have arranged it so that you won't pay a dime more for the expedited shipping, or if the gowns are a higher price. Can I place this new order for you?"

"Oh! My gosh!" most of them replied. "Yes, please go ahead. Thank you so much for taking care of this."

Phone call after phone call was mostly the same, until ...

"You're going to refund me all of my money. How could you trust a designer that you had to have known was going out of business?! What kind of business are *you* running?!"

One that cares enough to replace every single dress before I called any customers. One that spent an entire day trying to figure this out so you wouldn't panic.

"I don't trust you to fix this if you're going to trust a company like that."

Ouch. Fine. No problem. "Let me just ask my boss if it's OK to refund your five-hundred-dollar bridesmaid order." Like we had much of a choice!

After repeating the same message over and over again, I had to call the brides whose gowns weren't coming. This was a little different. Wedding dresses are more unique. There weren't any perfect matches to other designers' gowns.

"Hey, I'm so sorry for the news I'm about to deliver, but..."

"We can gift you our sample, and pay for your alterations to make it a size six instead of a size twelve ..."

"You can pick any gown in the shop and we won't charge you anything more ..."

"I'm so sorry to be the one to tell you, but ... we have a solution for this, but ... I have a fix for this, but want to know if it's OK with you to ..."

By the end of the day, my jaw was sore from talking. My head was buzzing with the sad delivery of the news that a hundred-year-old company was done for, and while most people were understanding that it was like predicting an earthquake, some were not so kind. I tried to brush it off. After all, the next day was a busy Saturday full of brides to serve.

Monday came. And the phone rang off the hook—it wasn't the brides or their maids, though. It was other stores.

"Do you have style number ..."

"I have Alfred Angelo gowns! Do you need any?!"

"My bride needs this bridal gown ..."

"I have a whole bunch of bridesmaids' dresses, but not the ones I need ..."

"What are you doing about ..."

I could help. I had that fresh new shipment of Alfred Angelo gowns delivered the week before. I had to help the brides across the country who needed these dresses.

A Facebook group was started, and I was fielding calls from brides who cried with relief when I told them, "Yes! I do have that wedding dress. I can ship it to you!"

The nightmare, the disaster, turned into a nationwide dress hunt. And I became the bridal angel who shipped all but a handful of the bursting-full boxes of dresses out to brides who needed them. The relief I heard on the phone was miraculous, "You're the tenth store I've called!"

I couldn't believe that the big box full of gowns turned into a saving grace.

The Alfred Angelo stores that were shuttered were snuck into by former managers who, despite the fact that they were now unemployed, grabbed their brides' gowns and drove them to their homes. We shipped out nearly fifty dresses. I folded each gown with loving care and slipped well-wishes into all the boxes I shipped out. I went from being the bearer of bad news to being the hero.

Then, *The New York Times* called me. They'd heard I had solutions to problems and could help. They were right. I did. And the article that was printed set me up for more and more calls, and I couldn't help but think:

If these brides needed to have good news given to them, I was the one to do that. I was the messenger who said "Yes" after their dreams were dashed. The calming presence that solved their problems before they even knew the problem existed. The divine change that allowed them to relax.

It's years later, and I am the owner of the store. And we veterans in the bridal industry talk about that day, Friday, July 13, 2017, as though we survived a war: "I survived the Alfred

Angelo disaster." And we did it because we care about every single "Yes" that resounds throughout the stores we love.

"Yes!" I always say now, no matter what the issue is. I'm happy to help. And happy to be the bridal angel for so many.

About Jillian

Jillian Forsberg is a bridal store owner and author with a master's degree in public history from Wichita State University. Jillian loves creating history in her shop with unforgettable moments that brides and their families can cherish for a lifetime, and every morning works on her historical fiction novels. Jillian can be found gardening, exploring antique malls, or reading every label at a museum. Vintage dresses are Jillian's clothing of choice, except when she's at the zoo. She lives in Wichita, Kansas, with her husband, child, and pets. She's currently working on her fourth novel and celebrating eighteen years in bridal.

Connect with Jillian
Facebook: Jillian Forsberg
Instagram, Threads, TikTok, and Pinterest: @jillianforsberg
info@jillianforsberg.com
Her shop: https://www.shopdressgallery.com
Read the *New York Times* Article:
https://www.nytimes.com/2017/11/01/fashion/weddings/the-bridal-shop-just-closed-how-to-rescue-the-day.html

Keep Going Anyway: Trusting God's Timing When Doubt Creeps In

Christine Furman

As I looked over my calendar pages each day, I remember feeling waves of anxiety rise in me—no blank space or break in sight. Every day was overscheduled, leaving little to no room to work on my business. Sure, it was full of activities for the kids and meetups with other moms, and I enjoyed those moments, but how was I ever going to gain traction in my entrepreneurial life? I had left my stable teaching career for this new life, and the stakes were high.

The dream to be home with my kids had become a reality, but bringing to life the business I envisioned—one where I could teach children, support other moms, and stay present with my own kids—proved to be more difficult than I imagined. On the outside, it seemed like I had everything I dreamed of: being home with my kids, not having to report to anyone but myself, and creating a schedule that best fit my life, but on the inside, I was stressed and overwhelmed. I enjoyed our park dates and connecting with moms, but during those conversations, my mind was constantly distracted by all the to-dos, not to mention the huge Momspiration412® event I was planning. This would be an opportunity for moms to connect while I entertained and engaged their kids through hands-on activities. It was approaching fast, and I had nothing ready for it!

As I shared my business vision with others, I was often met with encouraging responses: "This is such a great idea!"

"I would love to meet more mom friends."

"I wish something like this had been around when my kids were younger."

"How about we collaborate?"

While those words lifted my spirits, I honestly didn't know where to start. The vision and ideas came easily, but devoting time to the tasks and executing them was hard, especially with two kids under five and a husband who traveled for work. But because I'm ambitious (or maybe a little crazy), I teamed up with another business owner to host a huge family event—sponsors, vendors, activities, and the whole thing. I was used to hosting smaller events and engaging with families, but this time I bit off more than I could chew.

With only a few weeks left, I needed to reach out, organize activities, and invite more families to join. I'm not someone who typically struggles with anxiety, but I was feeling a panic attack coming on, especially once I found out my husband and parents would be out of town. How was I going to host this event with two littles in tow? I wasn't sure, but I was determined to figure it out. In 2020, about two weeks before the event, the world shut down during the COVID-19 global pandemic. Overnight, my calendar became wide open. The event I was unprepared for was postponed and eventually canceled. Whew! I was finally able to regroup, spend quality time at home with my children, Ella and Alex, and take the time God had granted me to plan and prepare more intentionally. I know this was a terrible time for many, but for me, it felt like I could breathe again.

Leading up to that moment, I had been waking up early every day, thinking I needed the time to work and complete tasks. But because I didn't have a solid plan, I was completely frustrated when the kids got up, already feeling behind. It was only 8 a.m., but in my mind, my day was practically over. I was exhausted and overwhelmed. I had left my teaching career to be present with Ella and Alex, not to be distracted and frustrated. At my peak frustration, I found myself wishing everything around me would pause—just long enough for me to catch my breath, analyze what I had gotten myself into, and reset it all. But I didn't know how to go from attending everything to clearing space in my calendar without disappointing someone.

Again, COVID solved that problem. When things shut down, Dan was out of town, and I was home with the kids. Although unsure of what to expect, I knew it was exactly what my heart, mind, and body needed: a break, a time to reset and figure out what truly mattered to my family. I was actually excited to stay home with my kids, having no pressure to attend anything. Finally, an opportunity to be present. No rushing out the door, cramming in activities, or filling every blank space on my calendar. As scary as things were outside our doors, I felt completely safe and at peace with my babies at home.

I quickly realized not everyone felt the same way. Many parents were panicking and unsure of what to do with their kids. They had to figure out how to teach their kids while also navigating the new challenge of working from home with them present. Schools were doing their best, but it was chaos, and most preschools shut down completely.

Ella's preschool shut down like so many others, but I wasn't too concerned. I basically had a full preschool setup in my home and had already been creating and teaching preschool curriculum. Before the pandemic, I was hosting in-person EduPlay® Learning events filled with hands-on activities and fun. Moms could connect while I engaged their kids with songs, educational games, stories, crafts, and themed snacks. When one of my business coaches asked for educators to go live online so families could work while the kids had a chance to learn and be entertained, I jumped at the opportunity.

I had imagined taking my events virtual years earlier but hadn't figured out how to make it happen. The pandemic made the transition feel natural, and the timing couldn't have been better. We were also moving to Augusta, Ga., and this gave me a way to continue serving my Pittsburgh, Pa., families while reaching new ones across the country and even around the world.

These daily live calls led me to go live in my rapidly growing Facebook group every day for three straight months. It became a way to offer families connection and normalcy during a time of so much uncertainty. Each morning, they'd tune in for "Start Your Day with EduPlay," where I led calendar time, movement, a story, and a simple activity using what they had at home. What started as a way to serve turned into so much more, including the opportunity to be a daily guest on 100.7 Star, a radio station. This was all happening while we were still in the middle of moving.

During all that momentum and excitement, a recurring vision surfaced—subscription kits for moms—hands-on learning delivered right to their doors. It was an idea that had been with me for a long time. A year earlier, I'd shared the idea with a business coach. I was excited to bring the idea to life, but instead of encouragement, I was met with resistance. She strongly urged me to focus on coaching instead, assuring me it was where the real profit would come from. While she may have been right from a financial standpoint, I knew I wasn't made just for coaching; I was made to teach. To connect. To support families in laying a strong foundation through hands-on, meaningful learning.

That conversation led to doubt and confusion. I questioned everything—my vision, my purpose—and I was unsure of my direction. Looking back, I can now see that what felt like a roadblock was actually God guiding my steps. He was preparing me for a time when families would need what I had to offer: hands-on learning, educational guidance, and all the necessary materials packaged together and sent directly to them. The pandemic was the perfect moment for EduPlay Learning Activity Kits to become a reality.

During 2020 and 2021, I connected with families across the globe. The move from Pennsylvania to Georgia went smoothly because I could go live, record videos, and teach from anywhere, and not just for my EduPlay students but for my own kids as well. The freedom I desired in my career and my family was finally becoming a reality. I stepped into full-time homeschooling and began helping families make education fun and meaningful at home.

It was also during this time that I began working with a mindset and marketing coach. With so many transitions underway, I wanted to avoid falling into old habits. I knew I needed to be intentional with my time, saying yes to things that lit me up and were aligned with my purpose, values, and family.

As families worked their way through their monthly activity kits, many began asking for help teaching their kids to read. This led to the development of the Reading FUNdamentals program—a fun, balanced approach to reading that builds both skill and confidence. As new ideas continued to flow, I kept creating, writing, and recording curriculum tailored to meet each family's unique needs. Providing curriculum and supplies was one part, but what was truly on my heart was offering individualized support to families as they navigated the twists and turns of home education. This desire ultimately led to the creation of the EduPlay Learning Academy, a space that empowers families to educate kids at home with the confidence that comes from having a teacher walk alongside them every step of the way.

Dreams continued to become reality. I was home with my kids, giving them the best education I could, and sharing that gift with others through a curriculum I had poured my heart into. Systems were falling into place. A consistent customer base was forming. I even started to build a small team.

But despite all the progress, overwhelm crept back in. Everything was happening so quickly. I often jumped from one project to the next without finishing the last. It's easy to fall into the people-pleasing mindset and try to do all the things. One day, I was completely frustrated. The endless to-do list piled up on my desk: videos to record, new curriculum to create, emails to read and write ... the list went on.

In my heart, all I wanted to do was teach my kids without all the distractions. I explained to my kids that I was ready to shut it all down. I wanted to close the business and just enjoy the life I had envisioned for us. Deep down, though, I knew that wasn't the calling God placed on my heart. I knew He wanted me to share these gifts with others, expand EduPlay Learning, and ensure no child fell through the cracks.

Later that afternoon, Ella handed me a note: "Please do not shut down the business. If you do, my kids will not be able to go to your academy. I LOVE you! Love, Ella." This simple, yet elegant response, from the heart of a child, was just what I needed to overcome the frustration and temptation to quit. It was clear that I was not only building this business for my children and the families I serve, but I was building a legacy for generations to come. It was also my reminder to slow down and tackle one task at a time without losing sight of what really mattered.

This moment was a prime example of the lesson I am reminded of over and over again—*keep going*! Are there going to be struggles and moments of doubt? Yes, but if you are truly following your calling, the resets will come when they are supposed to, the breakthroughs will be evident, and the next steps will fall into place one at a time.

It's not easy, though. I often think of the Tom Hanks quote from the movie, *A League of Their Own*, "If it wasn't hard, everyone would do it."[5] God has a bigger plan for your life than you can even imagine. We might have to encounter pain, frustration, overwhelm, and discouragement before His plan unfolds. I believe if you keep your eyes on Him, surround yourself with those who will lift, encourage, and support you through it all, there is nothing He cannot do.

I've had to pick myself up many times, feeling defeated and discouraged, but each time I can feel His presence saying *I am right here to lead and guide you every step of the way*. I truly believe it's my calling to provide resources and education to families, allowing them to meet their children where they are and provide them with an education that is fun, meaningful, and individualized. So I am going to keep going, lean on my faith, and embrace this life one moment at a time.

---

[5] *A League of Their Own*, performed by Tom Hanks(1992), https://www.youtube.com/watch?v=zyiQl2mDHsE

About Christine

Christine Furman, MEd, is a dedicated wife, homeschool mom, curriculum creator, podcast host, best-selling coauthor, and educator with over twenty years of experience in elementary and special education. Her passion for teaching has led her to develop and teach the EduPlay Learning Curriculum, which provides practical strategies, hands-on learning activities, and resources for families around the world. She is the host of the Home Education with Ease podcast, and her mission is to help moms raise lifelong learners and embrace a holistic approach to education at home. Christine has created supportive and encouraging communities in Pittsburgh, Pa., Augusta, Ga., and virtually for families passionate about raising kind, confident, and independent kids. As the CEO and founder of EduPlay® Learning and Momspiration412® Worldwide, she has grown a loyal following by being an expert contributor through radio, podcasts, TV shows, international stages, magazines, and family-oriented events.

Let's redefine what it means to educate your kids at home, ditch the stress, embrace the joy of learning, and set your family up for a lifetime of success!

Connect with Christine
www.christinefurman.com/welcome
christine@eduplaylearning.com

I Had a Plan

Denise Ann Galloni

I had a plan, and it was a good plan. But circumstances changed when I was laid off from my full-time job as a communications and leadership trainer, leaving me wondering what I was going to do.

A fellow trainer and mentor called to ask me if I wanted to work for a client who reached out to him for a short-term contract. The contract was only for thirty days, and I thought this would be perfect while I contemplated my next move. A few days after working with the client, they extended my contract to ninety days.

I had always thought about starting my own business, so no time like the present. In 2014, DG Training Solutions, Inc. (a corporate training and professional speaking company) was born. Since this one fell into my lap, I thought it would be so easy to find clients and have a successful business. I have a master's degree and have been working in the corporate world for a long time. I was a trainer for many years, so, of course, I thought I could do it for myself.

Anyone who has ever had the entrepreneurial bug will tell you it has its challenges. There is a learning curve, mistakes are often made, and times can be tough.

My first client ended up working with me for two years. It was a great experience, and I learned so much. The problem was that I didn't know how to find clients or what type of clients I was even looking for. I would work with anyone and adapted my business to each client; it was exhausting. After a few years, I realized this was not a great strategy. I didn't even have a business plan. Something had to change.

After my first two years of making a lot of money, the contract ended. I was so busy working with my first client, I didn't know how to get other clients, and I didn't have any in the pipeline. Months went by without any work, and the bills were accumulating. The clients were slim to none.

A few years later, I bit the bullet and started working with a new business coach. This man went from working in a video store to being on ABC's *Secret Millionaire*. The sky would be the limit if I learned from him and followed his suggestions.

When I first heard him speak, I felt an instant connection. He was from the Pittsburgh area, and after learning his story, I knew that this was the step I needed. I signed the coaching contract. It cost more money than I ever imagined spending on coaching.

He taught me so much, helped me pull my first book together, and introduced me to famous people who provided testimonials for my book—people like Kevin Harrington from *Shark Tank*, Joe Theismann (an American former professional football player), Brian Tracy (a well-known speaker and self-development author), and a few others. The trajectory was straight up for me and my rebranded business. I had a new mission, a brand-new and improved website, and a new sense of direction. I had a plan, and it was a good plan.

I remember having dinner with my family on New Year's Eve 2020, thinking 2021 was going to be the next great chapter of my life. I was beginning the third year of working with a coach and ready to implement everything I learned.

Little did I know the next chapter of my life would be nothing like I expected. The year 2021 would be the beginning of the worst three years of my life.

A few days into the new year, my sister called and told me there was something wrong with our mother. She seemed out of it. We took her to the emergency room, and they kept her overnight. When I went back the next morning to visit her, she had no idea where she was, who she was, or who I was. She was diagnosed with dementia. My mother, who was driving a few days before, suddenly could not remember how to walk.

My mother ended up going to rehab and did come home, but she was never the same, ever. At times, she did remember us and who she was, but as the months went on, those moments were few and far between. Then my sister had some medical issues, and it became difficult for her to care for our mother. I ended up staying with my mother and my sister twenty-four/seven for a few months.

This was a very emotional time. Not only did I have family stress, but I also had to juggle a full-time job and my growing consulting business. I had a plan, and it was a good plan. The plan was to have a successful consulting business, leave my full-time job, and travel across the world as a professional speaker. Would that have happened *if* my situation hadn't been altered because of my mother's diagnosis and other family members' health situations? I will never know.

I have always tried to avoid using the word *if*. It is such a small word, only two letters, with such a big meaning. *If* this or *if* that thinking is useless and can only cause more grief because you cannot change your circumstances, only how you react to them.

I did the only thing I could do to keep my sanity: I canceled upcoming commitments and put my business on hold. I had to focus on my family, my health, and keeping my full-time job (not knowing what the future would hold), all while sleeping on an air mattress at my mother's house for months.

You can only imagine the struggles of being a caregiver for someone with dementia or Alzheimer's. If you can't, let me help you understand. My day consisted of trying to work remotely while watching my mother constantly so she would not injure herself. Trying to get her to eat—anything—and then trying to get her out of bed. The worst part was her not remembering me.

Even though you know the person yelling at you and cursing at you is not the mother you've grown up with and known all your life, it still hurts.

After a year and a half of progressing dementia, she had an accident, and the dementia accelerated. A week later, she was gone.

Thinking things would go back to normal (the new normal), I had a plan, and it was a good plan. I was going to ramp up my business again. I needed to get back out there, networking and looking for opportunities. I thought it would be easy to pick up where I put my business down and keep moving forward. I wanted to get back to what I was thinking about that New Year's Eve a few years ago, when I felt incredibly excited about the future.

Sure, my new website was ready. I knew what type of clients I wanted to attract and what I wanted to focus my business on. Everything was the same ... wasn't it? Yes, except one thing: Denise Ann Galloni.

The past few years influenced me more than I could ever have imagined. I have always been a positive person and felt I could get through anything. I even founded the Positivity Circle, a monthly group that focused on inspiration, motivation, and positivity. But, I changed: my health was not the same, my weight increased from all the stress, and I felt hopeless for a while. I had to take care of myself. Focus on just me. It took time, but eventually I found that side of myself again, the one that was hopeful, excited, and motivated to succeed. I was done crying in the shower, hiding my tears so no one would know how upset I still was.

The trajectory of my life was changed forever. Changes occurred that were out of my control, but I had to ask myself, *What is my divine purpose? What is my new why? What is the plan?*

I have never been one to meditate. I can't sit still long enough and can't keep my mind from running rampant and thinking of a million things I need to do. I spent a long time just sitting in the quiet and doing nothing but thinking. I let my mind wander and just kept asking myself, *What do you want? What is important to you?*

It hit me like the proverbial light bulb in a comic, getting bright above my head. I didn't have to give up on my dreams. I had to modify them to the new Denise. The Denise who turned sixty years old. Yes, even that happened during this time, lol.

I had a plan, and it was a good plan. It was just a modified plan.

I decided to dust off my business and breathe new life into it. I could still do everything I wanted to do: have a successful business, bring on new clients, and travel the world speaking, just not all at one time.

I started to do podcasts to get myself back out there. I started to book speaking gigs. I called friends and colleagues I hadn't seen for a long time to touch base and let them know I was still out there working.

I started the Positivity Circle up again. It was dormant since the beginning of the pandemic. New members have been joining every month since. It feels great to focus on positive things and not the events I have no control over.

I rejoined some groups with people I missed so much. My television show won awards at the TV station's holiday banquet because I was focused on hosting great shows rather than just doing the show out of obligation.

I became an advocate for Alzheimer's and have a team that walks each year in the Walk to End Alzheimer's fundraising event. I was even interviewed by a local paper about my motivation and why I feel so strongly about fighting this horrible disease.

I put together my own anthology with eleven wonderful women telling stories about the aha moments that defined their lives. I had an incredible book launch showcasing these women and my third published book.

I agreed to be in the Course Corrected anthology when I heard the premise of the stories, dealing with changes and adversity and knew I had my own to share about resilience while dealing with family health issues, which will be my fourth published book.

And the biggest surprise to everyone who knows me—I decided to run for political office this year (2025), specifically for the local borough council. No one was more surprised than I was to find myself filling out the paperwork and throwing my name into the ring. Why? Someone asked me if I ever thought about running for local municipal council and told me what an asset I would be. After I thought long and hard about it, I decided, why not? Damn right I would be good at it, and I could make a difference, a real difference. But campaigning is a whole new experience.

I have a plan, and it is a good plan. My plan is to live each day the best way I can.

My life has never been the same and never will be since my sister called me that morning and said, "There is something really wrong with Mom." I never could have imagined the hell I would be in for those few years. But I also never would have imagined the people who stepped up and offered support and kindness.

I always knew I was strong (my family even called me the strong one), but I didn't feel strong; I felt weak and hopeless during those years. I was still strong, but not enough that I wouldn't break down and cry at a moment's notice. I can finally give myself some grace and know I handled everything the best I could.

I have a plan, and it is a good plan. My plan is family first; it is so precious the older I get and the smaller my family gets. Then myself, I need to remember to take care of myself. I am not there yet, but every day I get closer to being the Denise I used to be.

I am still campaigning for the upcoming election while getting my business back on track. There is no doubt in my mind I can do it all ... I've already shown myself I can over the past few years.

My divine purpose is to continue this new phase of my life and pursue my dreams—no, not dreams, but my goals. I have a plan for the future, and it is a good plan.

About Denise

Ever since being named "The Quietest Girl" in her senior class, Denise Ann Galloni has focused on using her voice and helping others find theirs. Working with organizations and individuals through her company, DG Training Solutions, Inc., Denise has delivered over five hundred presentations and keynotes to countless professionals who want to be better communicators and better leaders.

Denise's passion for leadership, communication, and corporate training has earned her a multitude of awards and recognition, including being a two-time distinguished Toastmaster and receiving the Business Choice Award for Corporate Training at the Pittsburgh Business Show. Denise's background in leadership and her desire to help others have led her to throw her hat in the political ring, running for Municipality Council of Bethel Park in the 2025 election.

She is the host of two award-winning TV shows, *Empowering You* and *Helping Hands*. Denise has been a featured guest on several domestic and international podcasts. She has been seen in over 100 media outlets.

Denise is the author of *Find Your VOICE: The 5 Keys to Lead and Empower Others* and a contributor to *Unleashing Your Soul-Level Magic*, a book that reached Amazon bestseller status in one day. Her newest book was released this spring (2025), *Steps to Success: One AHA Moment at a Time*, which became an Amazon bestselling eBook in three categories. Denise and James Malinchak, an in-demand business and motivational keynote speaker, who is one of the most requested, in-demand business and motivational keynote speakers and business marketing consultants in the world, cowrote the book *Success is a Choice: Inspiring Thoughts to Jumpstart Your Success*, due to be released in 2025, making *Course Corrected* Denise's fifth published book.

Denise received her master of science in professional leadership from Carlow University in Pittsburgh, Pa.

Denise regularly speaks for a variety of audiences (ranging from entry-level to experienced executives), for corporations, business groups, associations, and a variety of organizations.

When she is not hosting her TV shows, reading the new professional development book, or spending time with family, you can find her speaking in person and virtually to groups of twenty to over 20,000.

Any organization looking for an engaging speaker who will educate, motivate, and empower their audience to be better communicators and better leaders needs to book Denise for a keynote and/or workshop training today.

Connect with Denise
DeniseAnnGalloni.com
Facebook: Denise Ann Galloni
LinkedIn: Denise Ann Goodfellow Galloni

info@DeniseAnnGalloni.com

What I Couldn't Carry

Angela Goodman

The year I turned thirty-two wasn't a big deal to me. Life was the same day in and day out. I had no thought that life would change on a dime, but it did. I was deep into my second marriage with a daughter from my first husband and a career that kept me working seven days a week. I was attempting to prove I could accomplish everything and be the best, but it left me feeling empty, unappreciated, and unseen.

I attended school to earn a bachelor of science degree in chemical engineering from Virginia Tech, opened a construction startup with my first husband, began my career with Carrier Corporation, managed Showtimer's Community Theater in Roanoke, Va., and started pursuing my master's degree in business. All of this happened before I purchased my first home at the age of twenty-four. Nothing was stopping me, and I derived my value from my ability to juggle multiple tasks simultaneously.

After the birth of my first daughter in 2006 and subsequent divorce from her father, I soon found myself in love again with my soon-to-be husband. This catapulted me into a promotion at work since we could no longer work together while dating. Life was pushing hard and fast, and I was running away from everything. At this point, I was twenty-eight, experiencing a painful divorce, and looking for an exit plan from Roanoke. I didn't have a relationship with God at this time in my life, but I know now, He provided an escape hatch with the promotion to Chesapeake, Va.

In 2008, my second husband and I got married. I was happy at first, but the stress of having four grown stepdaughters and being in a new marriage was more than I could take. I was beyond overwhelmed. My oldest daughter was two years old at the time. My husband and I fought constantly. He struggled to find a new job in Chesapeake. To me, it seemed as if the only thing I could do right was throw myself into my career. I compartmentalized my life, focusing mostly on the relationships with my team at work. My daughter and husband had a strong relationship, and they spent lots of time together, often excluding me. I felt very lonely and isolated from my family. In my mind, I thought the only thing that would save us was having another child.

By the end of 2009, I had established myself as one of the top sales representatives in the commercial HVAC industry for our service business. I was mentored by some incredible executives who saw that I could outperform anyone. I was closing more than $2.5 million in sales annually in a market that only reached $3 million in total. I worked nonstop to be the breadwinner in our family, and I achieved it. I excelled in my career, yet at home, I felt like a failure and a terrible mother to my daughter. My ex-husband and I couldn't agree on anything. What was worse was that we fought in front of our daughter. It was bad, really bad. I often left these exchanges in tears and heartbroken, and it took years to forgive myself. The pain took my breath away. I had to control the situation, but in those moments, I was completely out of control.

The weight of life was heavy, and I was crying every day. I only wish I knew then what I know now—that I don't have to carry the weight alone. God does this for me today, and it's what God was trying to do then; I just didn't know it.

In the early winter of 2010, I was hoping to conceive but wasn't able to because of my birth control, so I decided to have it removed. I thought it might take some time to get pregnant. My husband had always wanted a boy, but had also made it clear that he wasn't sure he wanted another child because of his age. But when he committed, we tried everything. Less than a month later, I started to feel the early signs of pregnancy. My boobs hurt and everything I ate made me want to vomit. Maybe I would give him a boy after all.

By October of 2010, I was still working nonstop. I had closed several clients, including municipalities and a VA hospital, as well as other government contracts that required my problem-solving abilities, twenty-four hours a day, seven days a week. At this time, I was eight and a half months pregnant and definitely feeling the discomfort of carrying a small human in my body. My back pain was debilitating, and the only position I could sleep in had me boosted up on pillows in the bed, like a recliner. I would later find out this was not the best way to sleep. Throughout the final week of my pregnancy, I continued to scale ladders on job sites and worked nine to ten hours a day. I was very proud of myself because I could still do everything, and I was in control.

I gave birth to my beautiful baby girl in October, and everything was great until a few days after I got home from the hospital. I woke up one morning and tried to walk. It felt like there was a dagger stabbing me through my stomach; I was in excruciating pain. Fortunately, Scott was home with me because he had been laid off from his job. I called my doctor, and they told me to take a Percocet. In their words, "You'll be fine. You just had a baby." And I said to them, "This is my second child. I know what I should feel like after giving birth, and this isn't right." They told me to rest over the weekend and come in on Monday.

Over the weekend, the pain got progressively worse. I went in first thing Monday morning. My doctor's office was on the fourth floor, and once I made it up there, I waited. They put me into a room, and the doctor told me to lie on the bed. She performed various movements with my legs and hips. The pain felt like I was being gouged from the inside out, and I screamed bloody murder. She sent me for a CT scan, which was three blocks down the street. At the CT scan, they injected me with dye and completed the procedure. As I got into my car afterward, my phone immediately rang. It was the doctor's office. They said to me in a very terse tone that I needed to go back to the hospital down the street for another scan while the dye was still in my body. They needed another look. It was clear, in no uncertain terms, that I needed to go and go now.

The minute I arrived at the hospital imaging, they met me on the curb with a wheelchair. They rolled me back to the CT scan, and I remember the look on their faces: dark, dour, and frightened. They rolled me right past the waiting room and into the machine room. Within minutes, the scan was complete. I was rolled back out of the hospital and called the doctor from my car. They said, "Come back to the office right away, the doctor is going to come to the parking lot to talk to you."

Once we arrived in the parking lot, I called the office to alert them we were waiting—a newborn baby in the back seat and husband in the driver's seat. When I saw the doctor coming, I opened the car door. The doctor reached out and slammed it shut. (I didn't know why she reacted this way at the time, but I came to discover she didn't want me to get out of the car.) She gestured for me to roll the window down.

She said to me in a flat tone, "You're going to die."

I was in complete shock. She leaned in and said to me in a very matter-of-fact tone, "You have an ovarian vein thrombosis. I've already sent the admission paperwork to the hospital."

She looked at Scott and said something I'll never forget: "She's probably going to die."

The car was silent. I couldn't make sense of what she was saying. She continued as if what she said wasn't already going to make me go straight to the hospital. She was too factual, too crisp.

She again looked at Scott.

"You need to make sure when you get over there," she continued, "that they get her a wheelchair. Because if that thing moves, it'll go right to her brain and she'll be dead."

She looked me square in the eyes and said, "You're not going home to pack anything."

All I could manage to say was "OK."

Scott drove to the hospital in silence, one block over. They brought the wheelchair to the car, and I was loaded into it. They rolled me down a long, dark, endless hallway. I remember thinking to myself, "This isn't how it's supposed to end. I'm gonna see the other side of this." I was terrified yet true to my nature, still hopeful.

Once I had settled into my room, the doctor arrived. She said to me, "By the way, we also saw in the CT scan that you have a massive infection from your thighs to the top of your abdomen. The infection is attacking your organs. I will be starting you on IV antibiotics immediately."

I listened to what she was saying in disbelief. First, I was being admitted for a blood clot in my ovarian vein, now my organs were compromised by infection? The panic set in, and I started to cry. I was alone and scared. I didn't know how to feel or what to do. The next five days in the hospital were excruciating. I was a pin cushion between the injections for the blood clot and the IV.

Scott did his best to take care of our newborn while my dad was off gallivanting with some girlfriend somewhere. He never made it to see me. My mom was home taking care of my older daughter, and I didn't see her either. I attempted to continue producing breast milk and quit after the first day. I had failed as a mother ... again.

There was no surgery; they couldn't operate where the clot was located, so I was released from the hospital after the infection cleared. They taught me how to give myself injections before sending me home. For nearly two months, I didn't know whether I was going to live or die. No one could tell me my fate. I had to inject my stomach every morning and night with a blood thinner. When I went home, I was still in excruciating pain. The clot was cutting off circulation to the lower half of my body. When I moved, it pinched that artery in just the right way. The pain was like someone had taken a knife, stuck it in my abdomen, and twisted it. It shot through my entire midsection and down my right leg. It was six months before I was without that pain.

During this time, I was in a deep depression. I didn't really have any friends where we lived. I worked all the time. My much older neighbors brought food and checked in on me. My mom would come occasionally, but just to take my oldest over to her house. I assume it was also to assuage her guilt. My dad finally came to visit me; he claimed he didn't know how bad it was. That's his version of the story anyway. My father has always been very abrupt and cold. His inability to connect with me caused me pain for the remainder of our time in Virginia. I was having a hard enough time dealing with my physical challenges, but now I had to deal with the heartbreak of an absent father on top of it. Time passed, and in six months, we moved to Charlotte, N.C., where I got another promotion.

———

Looking back on this now, I'm surprised by how disconnected I was from who I am today and the role God played in carrying what I couldn't. I hope that I will never make the same mistakes again, but how can I be certain? It almost feels like this happened to someone else, yet I know it happened to me. Of course, I am supposed to tell you that I know it happened *for* me. And while I am grateful for it, I pray that God spares me this kind of pain in my life again.

Sometimes remembering this time catches my breath. I know what it was preparing me for now. I have a relationship with God, and it all started with this challenge. What I learned years later is that He was with me the entire time. I can also say now, no matter what I face, I never feel alone because I have Him by my side. I realize for some that may be too simplistic, but after all I have been through, I'll take simplicity and authenticity over complexity and chaos.

About Angela

Angela Goodman is a dynamic entrepreneur, community builder, and storyteller based in Ashburn, Va. After spending fifteen years engineering solutions in the buttoned-up world of corporate HVAC, she traded blueprints for brunch menus and launched Virginia's first Famous Toastery in 2016. Since then, she's been serving up sizzling success with a side of sass—and was even honored as the International Franchise Association's 2023 Franchisee of the Year (Yes, the eggs really *are* that good). She's also a founding partner of Valkyrie Ventures Group, where she works her financial alchemy to help others dissolve deep-seated money blocks, reclaim their worth, and step boldly into aligned abundance. Think of it as financial therapy with spreadsheets, soul work, and a whole lot of real talk.

But Angela didn't stop at flapjacks and French toast. She's also the visionary founder of EVOLVE, a soulful space where entrepreneurs, creatives, and seekers gather to rewrite their stories and reclaim their divine path. Through her podcast, *EVOLVE Thru God,* she invites listeners into real conversations about faith, healing, and those holy nudges that whisper, *There's more for you.* Spoiler alert: she answers them.

At home, Angela leads a wild and wonderful tribe that includes her two fierce and fabulous daughters, three rowdy dogs, and two cats who believe they own the place (and honestly, they might). Life under her roof is a blend of laughter, prayer, pet hair, and purpose—and she wouldn't have it any other way.

Connect with Angela

www.famoustoastery.com/ashburn
www.valkyrieventuresgroup.com
www.evolve-us.org

Who Am I Listening To?
How I Found Empowerment by Tuning Out the Noise and Trusting Myself

Tina Johnson

For years, I let the noise, the doubts in my head, the voices of others—that comparison game—hold me back from pursuing what I now feel is my true calling. I knew I wanted to empower women business owners. I wanted to make a real impact while building something meaningful. Yet, I couldn't fully step into the role I felt called to play.

For *two years*, I was paralyzed by impostor syndrome.

Not only was I struggling to map out how I could create a tangible business out of my soul's desire to help other women business owners, but I was also limiting myself by believing I needed certain credentials to be legitimate, even though I was already doing the work!

This is the story of how I broke out of that mindset trap, received divine inspiration that guided me forward when I was stuck, and learned to stop listening to the noise and start trusting myself. It's also about how I learned that through empowering others, I came to feel empowered, too. It's a story about how, despite the internal battles, I built a business that reflects who I *am*, not just what I do.

As a woman and a business owner, I've learned that empowerment doesn't come from waiting until you feel like "enough." It comes from taking bold, uncomfortable steps even when things feel uncertain. My journey hasn't been perfect, but it has been powerful! I hope by sharing it with you, you'll find a way to trust yourself and feel empowered to take the first step toward your divine dream, too.

Uncertainty After a Business Transition

After leaving a business partnership and surviving the uncertainty of COVID-19—and its devastating impact on my event management business of thirty-plus years—I found myself floating in a sea of uncertainty. The clarity I once had around my purpose felt blurred. I kept asking myself, *Am I making an impact?* I wanted to. Deeply. But I didn't know how to translate my desire to help women business owners into a viable business model.

I had a vague idea that I could be a business consultant (after all, I had been mentoring entrepreneurs for over a decade), but soon realized what I was doing was coaching. Yet the moment I thought about saying that out loud, the old stories came rushing in: *I'm not a coach. I don't have the credentials.* And even though I was already doing the work—supporting women, helping them grow, guiding their strategies—I didn't fully own the role. So, I delayed. For two more years, I danced around the edges of the business I knew in my heart I was called to do.

The truth is that impostor syndrome had its grip on me. I held myself back because I thought I needed someone else's permission—some outside "stamp of approval." But one day, in a moment of reflection, it hit me: I had over thirty years of experience running a successful event management company. I had built and led seven businesses before this. This wasn't a beginner's leap; it was my eighth venture! *Of course,* I was qualified.

I didn't need a certification to help women change their lives. I had *lived experience.* I had walked the path, made the mistakes, learned the lessons, and built a career and life around resilience, creativity, and business acumen.

Still, I couldn't shake the feeling that I was "dabbling" in coaching. I was doing the work, but without structure, without clarity, and with a lingering sense that maybe I wasn't qualified ... *enough.*

The Question That Changed It All

One day, I was having a conversation with my mentor, and she asked me a question that cracked something open inside me.

"At the end of the day," she said, "who are *you* listening to?"

That question hit hard because suddenly the answer was clear: I wasn't listening to *myself.*

I had spent years letting all those outside influences take the lead—the ones that said I wasn't educated enough, credentialed enough, or unique enough. The ones that whispered comparisons anytime I scrolled past the online presence of other coaches.

I had to face the truth, which was that the biggest obstacles weren't "out there." They were inside of me. I had to face my insecurity about not having a degree, my fear that I did not have a unique value-add in a saturated industry, and my hesitation to fully own what I knew I was capable of.

I had a choice to make. I could keep letting doubt run the show, keep shrinking, hesitating, and second-guessing. Or I could finally trust the voice inside me—the one that had been whispering all along, *You can do this*. I decided to start listening to my inner wisdom.

Divine Inspiration and the Birth of a Business

I knew what I wanted to do, who I wanted to serve, and why. I was ready to get my brave on. But I wasn't sure how I was going to make it happen. I prayed a lot ... for weeks. At a certain point, I boldly told God that He was just going to have to tell me how I was going to do this!

And, of course, He came through.

It was one of those three o'clock in the morning wakeups that you don't forget—the kind that feels more like a summons than insomnia. I got out of bed, grabbed my notebook and pen, and wrote down everything that came through to me without second-guessing the message. I can only describe it as an inspired stream of consciousness note-taking. My spirit was stirred, and a clear thought dropped into my mind like a pebble into water: *Create a program called FAB 5 to help five women in the five remaining months of the year*. This was in July of 2020, the year of COVID!

I didn't try to perfect an offering. I just followed the prompting, took a leap, and built what would become the CEO Consulting Group. The next day, I walked into the office and told my assistant, Cathy, that I was starting another business. She said, "Of course you are!" and we were off and running.

Within *two days*, five women said yes. Five women showed up ready to grow, ready to elevate their business success. That's when something in me clicked—I wasn't dabbling in this coaching concept anymore—this one leap became a launchpad. In 2021, I created the Women's CEO Business School, a year-long cohort for women to learn how to lead as the CEO of their companies, grow their businesses on their terms, and start to make a profit. That same year, we hosted the first annual Women's CEO Summit. And by 2023, we expanded again, launching the CEO Sisterhood, a nontraditional network group of powerful, like-minded women who support each other as women first, providing connection, guidance, and support. We also launched a full marketing division to serve our clients more holistically and have continued to set more supportive initiatives in motion year after year.

What began as a whisper in the night became a movement rooted in purpose and grounded action. I was finally building a business that reflected *who I was*, not just what I could do.

The Power of Belief

Seeing transformation in those first five women lit something inside me. Their breakthroughs became my confirmation. I watched these women step into their power, clarify their purpose, and shift their businesses (and lives) in real time.

I finally realized what I had resisted for so long: I *am* enough. I *am* qualified. And I *am* making a difference. A big one!

Take Nicole, for example, one of the original FAB 5 clients. Her story is a powerful testament to resilience, courage, and transformation. When we met in November 2020, she was balancing a demanding government job, a struggling marriage, and the full-time responsibility of raising three kids mostly on her own. At the time, she had just five clients and was making under five hundred dollars a month. Still, she had a dream: to build a business that could financially support her and her family, giving her the freedom to leave her job. She gave herself five years to make it happen, but deep down, she didn't believe it was possible. So, I told her I'd carry and believe in that dream for her until she could believe in it herself.

That day, we made a pact: If she committed to the process, put in the work, and trusted herself (and me), I knew we would bring her vision to life. And we did. In just three years. By December 2023, Nicole had built a thriving business, found the confidence to walk away from her marriage, and step into a life of independence and financial freedom.

Her story is a powerful reminder that transformation begins with belief, action, and the willingness to rewrite your narrative.

As my coaching business grew, so did my belief in myself, in the women I served, and in the ripple effect of empowered leadership. Mother Teresa once said, "I alone cannot change the world, but I can cast a stone across the water to create many ripples."[6] I feel the same, and it's a sentiment I live by. It's a privilege for me to see the ripple effect of one woman standing in her power and how that impacts her, her family, her community, and generations to come. There is a compound effect that extends from her own experience to the world at large. I am proud of these women and humbled that I get to be a part of their journeys.

I've learned a lot over these last few years—not just from building my different businesses, but from walking alongside so many women building theirs, and if there's one thing I know to be true, it's this: *Entrepreneurship is a calling, but it can be lonely.* We're expected to have answers, stay strong, and "keep it together." But behind the scenes, so many of us are tired. Questioning. Carrying way too much, silently.

---

[6] Quote by Mother Teresa,
https://www.goodreads.com/quotes/1109230-i-alone-cannot-change-the-world-but-i-can-cast

That's why women don't just need more strategy. They need *support*—wise, nonjudgmental, grounded support. They need space to reflect, reimagine, and make decisions that align with who they truly are.

Coaching, at its core, isn't about having all the answers; it's about helping others come home to their own answers. It's about creating a space where clarity, courage, and confidence can emerge organically. And here's another truth I've learned: You don't need a credential to do that. You don't need a polished bio or a fancy title or a degree. What qualifies you is your lived experience, your willingness to show up, and your heart to help others rise.

Listen to YOUR Voice and Validate Yourself

Helping other women find clarity helped me own *my* power. By creating the support I once needed, I became the woman I had been waiting for. That's the beauty of walking through doubt—you come out the other side stronger, steadier, and more rooted in who you are. I'm living proof that you don't have to have a five-year plan to get started. You can begin right where you are with imperfect ideas and shaky confidence. You can build as you go. You can trust that clarity will meet you on the path, but not before you take the first step.

As a child, my early years in foster care led to adoption into an abusive home, where trusting my inner voice was never encouraged, and affirmations of worth were absent. Self-doubt became a shadow, creeping in when I least expected it, and dimming my confidence. But I am learning to rewrite my story. I choose empowerment. I surround myself with love and support, distancing myself from voices that diminish me. I hold myself accountable by asking, *Is this thought an old wound or a new truth?* When doubt whispers, I challenge it: *Am I unfairly comparing my "chapter five" to someone else's "chapter fifteen"?*

Transformation doesn't happen overnight. But with daily habit changes—setting boundaries with those who don't uplift you, embracing affirmations, and living a daily life of gratitude—

the path to self-empowerment unfolds. Change begins within us. I challenge you to embrace your transformation today.

Let me leave you with the two questions that cracked everything open for me: *Who are you listening to?* and *What stories are you telling yourself that are keeping you stuck?* If those questions stir something in you, I invite you to take a step toward empowering yourself from within.

I've created a twenty-seven-page free digital self-empowerment journal that's filled with prompts and reflections to help you reconnect with your inner voice. The prompts and exercises will help you acknowledge the wisdom of your own experiences. They will provide a framework for creating a plan for how to surround yourself with people who truly see you and support your growth. And you'll identify the first, brave, imperfect step you can take toward your own inspired dream, *now*.

You can download the free journal here: www.theceowoman.com.

Remember, you don't need permission to begin. You already carry the wisdom you need. You are enough. *Start where you are.* You will grow into where you're meant to go. And I'll be here, cheering you on—because I believe in the ripple you're here to create.

About Tina

With over thirty-five years of entrepreneurial experience, Tina Johnson is a seasoned serial entrepreneur, certified business coach, and accomplished business growth strategist.

Driven by a passion to empower women business owners, she identified a critical gap in the coaching industry: Many entrepreneurs knew what needed to be done, but not how to do it.

In response, Tina founded the CEO Consulting Group and the Women's CEO Business School in 2020 to provide actionable strategies for building a sustainable business and achieving financial empowerment. In 2023, she launched the CEO Sisterhood, a values-driven community designed to foster authentic relationships and meaningful support among women entrepreneurs, moving beyond the limitations of traditional networking.

Tina is also the founder and CEO of JP Events & Consulting, an award-winning event management firm she launched over three decades ago. Under her leadership, the company has become a respected name in the Washington, DC, metropolitan area, producing premier corporate and private events.

Philanthropy is at the heart of Tina's work. A portion of every business transaction supports initiatives for women and girls. Based in Loudoun County, Va., she actively serves her community through various leadership roles, including cochair of the Women's Giving Back Capital Campaign ($4.5M goal), board director for the Loudoun Chamber of Commerce and the Loudoun Coalition on Women & Girls, and president of the Loudoun First Responders Foundation.

Tina has also held positions with Loudoun Interfaith Relief, Inc., Loudoun Abused Women's Shelter, National Association for Women Business Owners (NAWBO), Visit Loudoun, and the Medical Reserve Corps. Her dedication has earned her numerous accolades, including the George C. Marshall Award, NAWBO President's Award, Trailblazer Woman of the Year, Professional Service Business of the Year, and Entrepreneur of the Year.

Connect with Tina
Book a free strategy call: https://calendly.com/womens-ceo-business-school/strategy-call
Linkedin: @ceoconsultinggroupllc
Facebook: @CEOConsultingLLC
Instagram: @ceo_consulting_group_llc

Finding True Identity and Purpose: A Journey to Mental Health and Wellness

Judi Logan

"You're so dumb!"

"You're so stupid!"

"You're never going to amount to anything!"

"Who do you think you are?"

"You should never have been born!"

I took a deep breath and slowly let out a heavy sigh as my eyes fell to the ground. I once held my head high, my eyes bright with hope, until negative words pierced through my spirit like arrows. Agony and tears left me broken and defeated.

Have you ever felt the weight of similar words? Are you wearing labels that strangers, friends, or even family members have spoken over you? Perhaps you've become so accustomed to them that they've become part of your self-image, allowing those words to define who you are. That was me. I was there, swallowed up in a sea of shame and self-doubt.

My past led me through a maze full of twists and turns that had deception and destructive lies written all over it. I found myself calling on a God I wasn't sure was real. My journey would unravel so many levels of emotional pain, insecurities, and self-worth. So many labels and so many lies were spoken over me that I didn't know who I was anymore. I had no identity. I was lost, empty, and without a purpose. I felt utterly alone. Can you relate?

The familiar phrase "but God" signifies a pivotal moment in an individual's life where divine intervention overcomes a difficult or seemingly hopeless or impossible situation. These "but God" moments are significant among Christians worldwide because they acknowledge our human weakness, despair, and sin being transformed and redeemed by the power of God. "But God" is a huge part of my story; it represents the discovery of my true identity in Christ Jesus.

Genesis 1:27 reminds us that humans were created in God's image. We reflect His qualities, and we possess inherent worth and dignity. God is the ultimate authority on who we are because we were created by Him and for Him. He knows every hair on our heads (Luke 12:7), every tear we've shed (Psalm 56:8), and every prayer we've prayed (Psalm 34:17). God's viewpoint of us is all that matters—an audience of One. Our identity is not curated by our own thoughts or feelings or by the opinions of others. I carried the shame of my past for far too long, and it robbed me of my childhood and identity. Until one day, I found myself desperately seeking change. Desperate to find more in this empty world. Desperate to get more out of my empty life. The labels from my youth, the ones I started identifying with, would not determine my future. God wouldn't allow it. Even in desperate times, you can find three great spiritual virtues: faith, hope, and love.

In my desperation, I reached out to a God who accepted me just as I was: broken and empty. With His arms stretched wide, He makes himself real to us. This knowledge, this encounter, changed my life! God's love was bigger than the trauma I had experienced. I became a believer. When I heard that Jesus died for me on that cross, took away my sins and my shame, that's when I knew I was forever changed. That's when I knew that I was forgiven. I no longer identified myself as dumb or stupid—I have the mind of Christ (1 Corinthians 2:16). I no longer accepted that I wasn't going to amount to anything—God said that I have a purpose (Ephesians 2:10). And who do I think I am? I am a child of God (2 Corinthians 6:18). Psalm 139:13, "You made all the delicate, inner parts of my body and knit me together in my mother's womb" (NLT). I was meant to exist. All the lies and labels that were spoken over me were just that, "lies and labels." I stopped believing in the worthless words that had no value. They no longer carried the weight they once had, and I overcame the chains that kept me bound. I began to shed those lies. I discovered my true identity and purpose: my "but God" moment. This revelation sparked a journey of healing and growth. As I deepened my relationship with my Maker, I started to realize my purpose. My passion was loving people and helping others; that was my purpose and my calling.

The Holy Spirit would continuously nudge me to go deeper, to continue to learn more and seek more of Him to fulfill the calling He has on my life. With the Holy Spirit's direction, I felt led to go back to school. I was very nervous and unsure of my direction, but in the fall of 2021, I took a leap of faith and enrolled in ministry school. This was a three-year program to become an ordained minister. This was exciting, but very intimidating at the same time. What was I thinking? I was in my late forties and had been out of school for well over twenty years. I was never really good in school growing up, so how did I think I could do this all over again at this age? To write papers, reports, take exams, do presentations, and create sermons—who was I kidding? Past labels started to creep up to haunt me, reminding me that I could not do this. I was not smart enough for this. Facing my fears and past insecurities head-on, I held onto the truth that I am a child of God, equipped to succeed. I believed in the truth that God created me for more. I knew I could do this! My faith grew with every step I took toward my goals.

With dedication and perseverance, I was able to accomplish what my heart was set to do. I graduated with my ministry certification in 2022, received my ministry license in 2023, and was officially ordained as a minister in 2024. Simultaneously, in 2023, the Holy Spirit led me to write and publish my first book, a memoir titled *The Unraveling: My Story of Faith, Forgiveness, and a Family Restored.* My story tells of the goodness and faithfulness of my Savior, Jesus Christ. My book gives hope to the hopeless. Also, *The Unraveling* led me to become a number one bestselling author and has encouraged, inspired, and blessed so many readers (both believers and non-believers) worldwide, including myself. In 2024, as I was obtaining my ordination, I also pursued certification as a board-certified youth mental health coach. Obtaining this certification allowed me to better understand our youth today. My calling expanded, and I was driven by the desire to help women of all ages.

You might be asking, Why do all of this extra education? What are you doing with it? Good questions! First, this helped me see that no matter what labels you were marked with, you can do all things through Christ who strengthens you (Philippians 4:13). Second, my desire to help others stems from a global ministry called Beyond Survival Ministries (BSM), founded by Evangelist Sue Willis, whom I call my mentor mama. This ministry is special to me; it helped me confront and overcome the trauma that I had been carrying for most of my life and find healing through God's truth. It helped me to "frame my story in redemption," as Pastor Sue would say. A specialized small group program within the ministry called A Time to Heal Beyond Survival (ATTHBS) allowed me to heal my spirit, soul, and body. I was searching for the truth, and God's truth is what I received, transforming my pain into purpose.

Words shape our individuality. Words hold immense power, both to build up and tear down. We often don't realize the impact of the words we speak, causing them to hurt people rather than heal them. Ephesians 4:29 reminds us, "Don't use foul or abusive language. Let everything you say be good and helpful, so that your words will be an encouragement to those who hear them" (NLT). Our words should be helpful, meant to build up and empower others to walk worthy and in step with God's will for their lives. Our words should provide encouragement and God's truth spoken in love. Our words should also be beneficial, adding value to the lives of those who hear them. Just like nutritious food gives life to the body, wholesome words that heal and help give life to the soul.

As part of the core team for BSM, I serve as a certified leader and trainer for ATTHBS small groups. This is where I use my calling to minister to the hurt and broken. Because I once was in their shoes, I can help hurting individuals reclaim their lives, find healing through God's truth, and ignite the God-given purpose burning inside of them. The goal is not to marinate in the trauma, but to make known what God has done in their lives, allowing beauty to grow out of ashes, reclaiming the life that they once thought was too far gone, aiding them in their journey of hope, healing, and restoration, and watching their lives be transformed by the Word of God. This process not only ministers to them, but ministers to me as well, as I see the work of the Lord in an individual's life. It is so refreshing and such a freedom to see people's lives change—their "but God" moments. He brings good out of evil; there is hope. "Now may the God of peace Himself sanctify you entirely; and may your spirit and soul and body be kept complete ..." (1 Thessalonians 5:23 NASB).

While ministering to people's hearts and souls, I recognized the need for holistic healing. This realization led me to become a Mary Kay consultant to help women regain confidence in their appearance, complementing their inner healing. Additionally, I came across a company called THREE International. THREE International is a proactive, holistic wellness company, specializing in health and nutritional supplements that utilizes advanced cellular absorption technology to advance bioavailability and overall health benefits. This company was a game changer for me.

I was suffering from plantar fasciitis, an inflammation of the fibrous tissue (plantar fascia) along the bottom of my foot that connects my heel bone to my toes.7 I was in excruciating pain, not just in one foot, but both feet. Sadly, all the stylish shoes I once wore were now a fleeting thought. The final accessory to my wardrobe was diminished to gym shoes with custom orthotics for cushion and support for my feet. I hated this. I felt incomplete, my confidence level shot. You don't realize the boost of confidence you gain when your outfits, shoes, and accessories come together. It's huge!

---

7 https://www.mayoclinic.org/diseases-conditions/plantar-fasciitis/symptoms-causes/syc-20354846

I was introduced to a product called Revive, which supports healthy joints, eases muscle stiffness, reduces inflammation, and counteracts the effects of free radicals. It's holistic and only made with pure ingredients. I thought I should try it, since I was desperate to feel better, and because nothing else that my podiatrist recommended actually worked. And I was not about to get cortisone shots in my feet that would last only a month or two. Ouch! I tried Revive, and within two months of taking it daily, the pain completely went away. I couldn't believe it! Just like that, I was completely healed, no more pain. It was amazing! And I felt great again, especially since I could now wear the stylish shoes I wanted.

I researched the company further and discovered their approach to wholeness. What started as a cure for the plantar fasciitis I was experiencing led me to a whole new world of proactive wellness, reminding me that healing touches every part of life: mental, spiritual, and physical. One by one, I started taking the supplements they offered. I discovered that I was able to sleep better, go to the bathroom regularly, reduce bloating, increase my energy and mental clarity, and look a lot younger than my true age! Not only did I feel good, but I looked good as well. I remember my friends and even strangers I encountered would say to me, "You look so young, what's your secret?" or "With five kids and all that you do, where do you find the energy for it all?" Once I saw the difference it was making in my own life, I knew I had to share this secret with my family, friends, and everyone I encountered. My goal is to add value to people's lives in their overall mental health and wellness.

This journey—from brokenness to wholeness, from doubt to faith—has made me feel complete and well-equipped in my mission and calling to help others achieve wellness (physically, mentally, and spiritually), ministering to the whole person. Because I worked to overcome the words that held me back years before, now, I get to encourage people to discover their true identity and purpose in Christ, while keeping their body (the temple of the Holy Spirit) healthy in the most balanced and fulfilling way. Ultimately, I have found purpose in helping others by enhancing overall wholeness and quality of life. With God's guidance, I help individuals look and feel their best, both inside and out. Hope is attainable, and new beginnings are available to those who hunger for it. Absolute freedom—being happy, healthy, and whole—is worth the journey.

About Judi

Judi Logan is a proud mother of five amazingly talented children, along with her new bonus daughter-in-love. She lives in Pennsylvania with her husband, their kids, and their sweet Aussiedoodle, Asha. An ordained minister, Judi serves faithfully at her local church, revival meetings, women's conferences, and through community outreaches across Pittsburgh and beyond. Her ministry is deeply rooted in her own powerful story, using her journey of healing, resilience, and redemption to inspire others to embrace self-love, to freely forgive others, and to find healing and hope through a relationship with God.

Outside of ministry, she is a best-selling author, speaker, teacher, and business owner. Judi treasures quality time with her family and friends and finds joy in the simple things, especially discovering new restaurants and sharing meals with loved ones. A passionate foodie, she's known for taking mouthwatering photos of dishes that are almost too good to eat. But more than the food, she's about the people; she captures meaningful moments and cherishes every person she meets along the way, creating lasting connections.

Judi's warmth, authenticity, and unwavering faith shine through in everything she does. To know her is to feel seen, loved, and encouraged ... and once you meet her, you've made a friend for life.

Connect with Judi
http://mybestself.threeinternational.com
http://marykay.com/jlogan818
http://beyondsurvivalministries.org

From Lip Gloss to Laparoscopes: Life Before the Full Frontal

Dr. Sheri Mancini

If you had told my teenage self—circa big bangs, Aqua Net, and a diary full of angst—that I'd grow up to become a surgeon and a health coach, she would've rolled her eyes, lit a cigarette, and cranked the volume on her cassette Walkman. My adolescence played out in a time before texts and Instagram drama—we called each other (from landlines), hung up on boyfriends for dramatic effect, and passed folded-up notes like they were sacred scrolls. We snuck wine coolers into school dances, smoked in hiding, and treated every crush like it was the end of the world. Idiots. Lovable, emotional, over-perfumed idiots.

And while I cringe now, I have to give her a break. Neuroscience has my back: the frontal lobes—the part of the brain responsible for impulse control, long-term planning, and the ability to say, *This is a bad idea*—don't fully develop until your mid-twenties. I like to think I was living life pre-full frontal. Not in the scandalous sense, but neurologically speaking.

This story is about switching things up. About how a girl once ruled by hormones, heartbreak, and half-developed brain matter eventually found herself holding a scalpel, guiding others toward better health, and—most surprisingly—enjoying it. Turns out you can reinvent yourself.

So it tracks that someone operating on partial brainpower made a few questionable choices. And yet, I became a surgeon. And later, a health coach. I spend my days helping others navigate their health with clarity and purpose—tools I didn't have back when I was dodging curfews and wearing Jordache jeans.

Speaking of Jordache jeans (ooh, and Gloria Vanderbilt!), I didn't grow up with money. We weren't starving, and we always had a roof over our heads and food on the table—meatloaf, fish sticks, TV dinners on metal trays—but we were undeniably broke. The stress around money wasn't subtle; it lived in the walls. I remember my mom standing at the kitchen counter, bills spread out like landmines, quietly crying as she did the math. She worked two jobs after the divorce to keep us afloat, and even as a kid, I knew how heavy that burden was.

We didn't have extras. We had a patched-up, barely operational Plymouth Arrow that wheezed down the road like it needed a pep talk. If it started on the first try, it felt like a small miracle. But that car got us where we needed to go—school, jobs, the store—and somehow, that was enough. Just barely, but enough.

And still—I'm grateful. Grateful I learned early how to stretch a dollar, appreciate what I had, and recognize hard work when I saw it. That tightrope walk of not-quite-enough built grit, compassion, and a deep respect for anyone who keeps showing up when life doesn't hand them an easy path. It taught me that you can be broke without being broken. That you can have very little and still grow up with everything that matters.

That kind of environment—tight money, a working mom barely holding it all together—planted something in me early: a quiet, relentless determination to succeed. I knew I wanted more—not in a material way, but in a stability way. I wanted to build a life where I didn't have to cry over bills at the kitchen counter. I was good at science. I made good grades. And somewhere along the way, I realized: I wanted to be a doctor. The kind that no one in my family had ever been.

There was just one problem—medical school is expensive. Really expensive. So I did what scrappy, determined kids from modest beginnings do: I found a way. I joined the military. The Navy gave me a scholarship to pay for medical school, and I gave them years of service in return. It was a deal I made proudly. It was the launchpad that took a broke kid from a small house with meatloaf dinners to being the first doctor in the family.

I loved being a surgeon. Still do. From the moment I picked up a scalpel, it felt like home—like I had stepped into the life I was built for. I was good at it, and I loved the intensity, the problem-solving, the precision. Surgery was my calling. It still is.

But about twenty years in, something started to shift—not in me, but around me. The U.S. healthcare system, bloated and broken, had turned into a bureaucratic maze. Less time with patients, more time clicking boxes, coding visits, and playing phone tag with insurance companies. I coped by becoming something of a virtuoso complainer. I wrote novels in email form to hospital leadership, pointing out everything wrong with modern medicine, like I was submitting op-eds to the New England Journal of Frustration. Spoiler alert: it wasn't particularly helpful. I was burning out, and venting—even eloquently—wasn't enough to fix it.

That's when I pivoted. I stepped back to part-time surgery and did something that, even to me, felt ironic: I became a health coach. After two decades in the OR treating the consequences of poor health, I was suddenly on the front lines of prevention. One-on-one. No insurance companies. No prior authorizations. Just me, helping people—often family and friends—transform their lives before they ever needed an operation. It was refreshing. It was personal. And in its own way, it brought me back to why I started in the first place: to make a difference.

Looking back, it's hard not to laugh—and wince—at the girl who smoked behind the school, cried over boyfriends, and rode shotgun in a Plymouth Arrow held together by hope and duct tape. But every awkward note, every dollar stretched, every late-night anatomy cram session, and early-morning surgery shaped the woman I became. And just when I thought the story was fully written, I found space for a new chapter. Reinvention didn't mean walking away from who I was—it meant building on it. I'm still a surgeon. I'm still called to heal. But now, I get to meet people earlier in their journey. I get to cheer them on, teach them to care for their health, and remind them that change is always possible.

Full frontal lobe finally online, I'm using it to do exactly what that dramatic teenage girl never could've imagined: guide others toward health with clarity, compassion, and a whole lot less Aqua Net. I remember what it's like to feel out of control, to cope poorly, to make decisions from the part of your brain that isn't logical. And because of that, I don't coach from a pedestal. I coach from a place of been-there, messed-that-up, got-the-growth. Turns out all those cringeworthy detours weren't wasted. They gave me the map.

About Sheri

Sheri Mancini, MD, is a board-certified general surgeon and certified Optavia health coach. A graduate of the University of Pittsburgh School of Medicine, she earned her degree with honors and received a Navy scholarship to fund her training. In the Navy, she served as the ship surgeon on an aircraft carrier during Operation Enduring Freedom. She was also deployed to provide medical support for the United States Marines during Operation Iraqi Freedom. After more than two decades in the operating room, she now blends surgical expertise with preventive coaching, helping clients take control of their health before disease takes hold.

She lives with her husband and two children, along with a lively crew of animals—including a dog, cat, bunny, backyard chickens, and a beehive. Energetic and deeply grateful, she believes in living with intention, embracing reinvention, and saying yes to life whenever possible.

Connect with Sheri

https://www.facebook.com/sheri.mancini
https://www.instagram.com/sherimancinipgh/

When We Listen

By Dr. Leslie Pasco

When I was seven years old, I had an experience that I believe was a divine encounter. I was lying down for a nap in my childhood bedroom, my eyes lazily tracing the familiar patterns of the wooden dresser across from my bed. A bright light seemed to fill the room, and then suddenly, the wood grain seemed to shift and coalesce, forming the image of a face.

It was the face of Jesus.

His features were not perfectly clear, but they were unmistakable—the gentle eyes, the serene brow, the flowing hair. And his lips were moving. Although I couldn't hear any sound, I instinctively knew he was speaking to me.

While I could see he was filled with light and love, for some inexplicable reason, a wave of fear washed over me, and I instinctively squeezed my eyes shut. When I finally mustered the courage to open them again, He was gone.

The experience was brief, lasting only a few moments, yet it left an indelible mark on my soul. I lay there in the stillness of the room for what felt like an eternity, my mind racing, trying to make sense of what had just happened. What did Jesus want with me? I knew in my heart that He was giving me a message, if I had just listened, but ...

I wasn't ready to listen.

I always wanted to be a famous artist. The kind of famous artist who lived in New York City on the top floor of a fancy building, going to art parties with snobby friends, drinking expensive champagne, and eating chic food. Even though I grew up poor, I had big dreams and expensive tastes, knowing that I would do something important, meaningful, and impactful with my life.

Statistically, I knew that very few artists would make it to fame and fortune. This led me to question whether pursuing art at the risk of poverty was worthwhile, or if I should choose a career more likely to support the lifestyle I dreamed of. Exploring my options, I decided to study medicine and quickly switched my major to the sciences. As I put down the art pencils and picked up a scalpel in the anatomy lab, I found myself considering becoming a heart surgeon, but the long hours, being on call, and intense rotations prompted me to consider my options, yet again.

As I reclined in the dental chair for my semiannual appointment, the sounds of drills and suction replaced by the rhythmic hum of my own thoughts, I found myself pondering my career trajectory. The dentist, who I thought was all swagger and no heart, noticed my distant gaze and inquired about my thoughts. Caught off guard by his genuine concern, I found myself confiding in him about my career uncertainties.

He listened patiently as I described my anxieties and aspirations, offering sympathy and gentle encouragement. After boasting about his Jaguar and mansion, he suggested that I consider a career in dentistry. It was perfect for females who may want to eventually start a family, he said. To give me a glimpse into the daily life of a dentist, he invited me to shadow him for a day at his practice.

Part of me wondered if his offer was motivated by genuine interest in my future or simply a flirtatious ploy. After all, he was known for his charm and had a reputation with the ladies.

Despite my initial reservations that a career in dentistry would be repulsive, my intuition urged me to accept his offer.

I listened.

I knew I had made the right decision only minutes into shadowing my mentor's first case of the day. He had transformed a middle-aged woman's smile, and as she looked in the mirror, tears welled up in her eyes, and her self-worth was restored. Witnessing the powerful impact that the combination of art and science had on her emotions solidified my belief that a career as a dentist would be both meaningful and impactful.

I was fortunate enough to be accepted early into dental school, a rigorous and demanding program where I dedicated four years of my life to intensive study and clinical training. During this transformative period, I not only gained a deep understanding of dental science and honed my clinical skills but also forged lifelong friendships with my fellow students. These bonds, built on shared experiences and mutual support, have continued to enrich my personal and professional life long after graduation.

For a significant period, I derived immense satisfaction from my profession as a dentist. The ability to alleviate the pain and suffering of my patients, to improve their oral health, and to contribute to their overall well-being was deeply gratifying. The knowledge that I was making a tangible difference in their lives, not just through the technical aspects of my work, but also through the relationships I built and the trust I earned, was incredibly fulfilling.

Witnessing the transformation in a patient's smile after a procedure, or hearing about how their improved oral health had boosted their confidence and self-esteem, reinforced the value of my work. It wasn't merely about fixing teeth; it was about improving lives. The positive impact I had on their lives extended far beyond the dental chair, and that was what truly made my work meaningful.

While I didn't live on the top floor of a fancy building and hang out with snobby friends, I did much better than I had ever expected. I had a beautiful new home in the neighborhood I always dreamed of living in, and I went to many upscale parties that served champagne and chic food. Life was good.

Over time, however, the demanding nature of being a practitioner and running my own dental practice, coupled with a particularly challenging and negative patient experience, began to take its toll. The stress and pressure gradually eroded my initial enthusiasm, leading to self-doubt and a growing sense of disillusionment.

I found myself trapped in a labyrinth of doubt, questioning the very essence of continuing my career choice and contemplating a drastic shift in my professional trajectory. The once unwavering confidence I held in my chosen path had been replaced by a gnawing uncertainty that permeated my thoughts and actions. I was in a dark place, but it was during this period that a profound introspection took over, and I came to the stark realization that my understanding of the human experience was woefully incomplete. While my rigorous dental training had equipped me with an extensive and specialized knowledge of oral health and its intricate complexities, I had inadvertently neglected the profound and inextricable connection between people—a connection that underpins the very essence of human existence.

During this turmoil and amidst a sea of papers, a seemingly insignificant mailer on my desk caught my attention. It beckoned me to explore uncharted territory, to delve into the realm of human connection. It was about managing a dental practice, but the message it conveyed resonated with an unspoken yearning within me, a desire to bridge the gap between my clinical expertise and a more holistic understanding of the individuals who sought my care. Although darkness threatened to consume me, I refused to succumb to its suffocating embrace. Instead, I chose to pay heed to the subtle signs, recognizing them as beacons guiding me toward a more enlightened and fulfilling path.

I listened.

Driven by a renewed sense of purpose, I embarked on a journey of self-discovery and professional growth. I delved into the study of human behavior and the intricate relationship of human connection. Through my study, training, and continued work with patients and my practice, I came to appreciate the significant impact of good communication and the role it plays in developing human relationships, with others and ourselves. Delving deeper into my studies, I discovered the intricate relationship between the mind and body, and how profoundly our mental and emotional states can influence our physical health and well-being. The mind, it turns out, is not just an abstract entity separate from the body, but rather an integral part of our overall being, with the power to shape our physiological processes, immune responses, and even the structure and function of our cells.

For example, chronic stress, anxiety, and negative emotions can trigger a cascade of physiological changes, including the release of stress hormones, increased inflammation, and suppressed immune function, which can contribute to a wide range of health problems, from heart disease and digestive disorders to autoimmune diseases and cancer.

On the other hand, positive emotions, mindfulness practices, and a sense of inner peace can have a restorative and healing effect on the body, promoting relaxation, reducing inflammation, and boosting the immune system.

This mind-body connection highlights the importance of taking a holistic approach to health and wellness, one that addresses not just the physical symptoms of disease but also the underlying mental and emotional factors that may be contributing to them. By cultivating positive emotions, managing stress, and practicing mindfulness, we can harness the power of the mind to promote healing, enhance resilience, and achieve optimal health and well-being.

I listened.

Knowledge is power, but with that power comes great responsibility. When we gain understanding, insight, or expertise, we hold the ability to influence outcomes, shape lives, and drive change. It's up to each of us to use that knowledge with integrity, compassion, and purpose—not just for personal gain, but to uplift others and contribute to a better world. True wisdom lies not just in knowing, but in doing what is right with what we know.

One day, as I was debating about retiring, a seemingly ordinary moment transformed into an epiphany. As I sat in my daughter's orthodontist's office, surrounded by other parents, a conversation between two mothers captured my attention. They were discussing their children's orthodontic treatment plans. One mother detailed her son's upcoming radical and painful jaw

114 | Course Corrected

surgery, a necessary procedure to correct his bite. The other mother, her voice filled with conviction, urged her to explore myofunctional therapy as an alternative.[8] She recounted her own daughter's success with the therapy, emphasizing its effectiveness in promoting proper muscle function and jaw development.

As I listened to their exchange, a wave of emotion washed over me, leaving me breathless and overwhelmed because I had secretly been considering exploring myofunctional therapy as an alternative to retirement. But retirement had been tempting me, and I wasn't sure what to do. My body tingled with an exhilarating mix of excitement and anticipation, and tears of joy welled up in my eyes, blurring my vision. In that singular moment, amidst the cacophony of thoughts and emotions, I felt a profound sense of clarity and purpose. It was as if the universe had conspired to deliver a divine message, unequivocally affirming that I was on the right path. Every doubt, every insecurity, every lingering fear dissipated, replaced by an unshakeable conviction.

I listened.

A newfound determination—a vibrant current of purpose—surged through my veins, compelling me forward. A clear vision took root: to champion the healthy growth of children's jaws and airways. With an unwavering resolve, rather than retiring, I committed myself to the intricate world of orofacial myology. The path ahead, I knew, wouldn't be a gentle stroll; it would be fraught with challenges and many obstacles. Yet, armed with the profound knowledge of my purpose, my spirit remained unyielding, a steadfast flame against the winds of doubt. The initial spark of inspiration had blossomed within me, unfurling into a resolute determination. Eagerness pulsed within me—a desire to share the fruits of my work with the world—to weave my people skills, business acumen, and medical knowledge into

---

[8] https://my.clevelandclinic.org/health/treatments/myofunctional-therapy

a sanctuary dedicated to nurturing the jaw and airway development of children.

Driven by an unwavering conviction, I made a decisive break. I sold my thriving dental practice and set aside the comfortable vision of a predictable retirement. A new endeavor beckoned: the creation of a myofunctional therapy center, a haven built upon proven methods to guide children from their earliest years toward proper jaw development and healthy breathing. The profound belief resonated within me: if children grow and breathe correctly, they unlock the potential for a richer, healthier life, a life hopefully unburdened by medications and breathing machines. This could change healthcare as we know it.

Today, I am pioneering a new way to help children grow right, breathe right, and live better—the way God intended for them.

Throughout my life, a profound question had lingered: was my divine encounter with Jesus a genuine reality or merely a figment of my imagination? Today, the answer has softened in its importance. Whether the experience was objectively real or not has become secondary to the undeniable truth it revealed within me. I now believe, with an unwavering certainty, that my experience was a genuine divine encounter, a moment where Jesus spoke something extraordinary into my being. But what resonates most deeply now is the profound sense of listening, of heeding a call. I understand that the power and gifts I have been given are not mine to hoard. They are instruments to help our world, His world, blossom into a better place for all of us.

Listen.

About Dr. Leslie

As a general dentist for over twenty-five years, a dental consultant, and a professional speaker to the healthcare industry, Dr. Leslie has experienced the dental profession in almost every way. In treating hundreds of thousands of patients over her career and observing a serious health pandemic afflicting our population, Dr. Leslie, also a trained orofacial myologist and Certified Buteyko Breathing Instructor, is now dedicating the remaining years of her career to providing myofunctional therapy options to help children grow and develop their jaws and airways properly, so they can breathe right and live better for a lifetime.

Connect with Dr. Leslie
www.myowaycenters.com

https://x.com/DrLesliePasco
https://www.youtube.com/@MyoWayCentersforKids
https://www.linkedin.com/in/dr-leslie-pasco-03a096a1/
https://www.instagram.com/myoway_centersforkids/
https://www.facebook.com/people/Myoway-Centers-For-Kids/61558102876773/

When the Worst Thing Becomes the Best Thing

Sally Power

I know what it's like to hit rock bottom. I also know that sometimes, when your life feels like it's falling apart, it's really falling into place.

There was a time when everything looked picture-perfect. I married the love of my life—a tall, dark, and handsome man I met at church. It felt like a fairy tale at first. But like so many stories, there was more going on behind the scenes. I didn't know how broken he really was. I didn't know about the demons he was fighting—demons that would take years to fully come to light. Addiction. Alcohol. Lies. All hidden so well … until they weren't. I didn't recognize how broken I was. I could have been the poster child for codependency, trying to keep my husband and everyone else happy and saying what I thought they wanted to hear. I tried to do more—be more—keep it all together. The combination constructed a house of cards that came tumbling down when the pressure got too great. After twenty-plus years of marriage, we had three beautiful children—two boys and a girl in their preteen and teen years. By the time my husband left, he was bitter and angry; he never returned. He drove away in his construction van packed to the brim with all his worldly possessions, and I was left—a broken single mom with three kids who were likewise bruised and angry.

The wake of destruction was not just emotional. I was left with over $200,000 in debt. Despite being well-compensated as a full-time teacher and doing my best to juggle life on my own, I was still coming up short by three hundred to four hundred dollars every single month. From the outside, we looked like your average suburban family. But behind our front door, I was counting pennies and carrying the weight of it all.

To be perfectly honest, I felt like a failure. I couldn't afford pizza nights. I couldn't give my kids what other kids had. I was tired. I was angry. And I knew I was not as emotionally available for my kids as they needed me to be. I was in function mode, and I was weary of being the "crummy mommy."

In that place of brokenness and desperation, I knew I had to do something. I had nothing left to lose and just enough grit to grasp for something new. With the last of my resources, I secured a tiny consignment store to supplement my teaching income. It was only open three days a week, and two of my friends (very dear friends) ran the shop for free while I continued teaching full-time. I could not have done it without them; it was exhausting doing it *with* them! We pressed through with the hope that this would bring just enough revenue to keep my head above water.

Then, one day, something happened that changed everything.

I wasn't in the shop that day, but my dear friend Jackie was. A young woman came in, clutching a gift certificate from a local domestic violence agency. She looked defeated: shoulders slumped and eyes downcast. That gift certificate was all she had. She had fled an abusive relationship with literally the clothes on her back.

The woman sheepishly shared her dilemma, and Jackie never missed a beat.

"How 'bout some jammies?" Jackie helped her pick out some jammies, oversized sweaters, and jeans—double the value of the gift certificate. When the woman walked out of the store, her whole countenance was transformed. She stood taller, her eyes sparkled, and there was a spring in her step. She left with the hope that tomorrow could be a better day!

When I heard the story later that day, I sat down and cried.

That was the nudge. The whisper. The holy shove. That was the moment I knew this store wasn't just about clothing—it was about hope. It was about waving a magic wand, changing the outward appearance, and releasing the treasure within women like her (and like me), and letting them rise from the ashes.

That's how Treasure House Fashions (THF) was born.

With the help of a few generous businessmen, I secured nonprofit status. I enlisted my sister Cindy and other fierce, like-hearted women, and together, we began building something much bigger than a resale shop. We built a mission.

Our mission is simple: *to promote the dignity and self-esteem of women, particularly women in transition or crisis. Outward appearance is not an accurate reflection of your worth, but it can affirm the treasure that you truly are.* Even when everything feels lost, I believe each woman is still a pearl of great price.

Looking back, I can say this with complete certainty: *The worst thing in your life can become the best—when God's hand is in it.* He took my mess and turned it into my message.

Today, Treasure House Fashions works with over sixty agencies across Pittsburgh—places like the Allegheny County Jail, Gateway Rehab, Crisis Center North, Light of Life Rescue Mission, Women's Shelter and Center of Greater Pittsburgh, and many others. We help women who are coming out of jail, fleeing abusive relationships, fighting through addiction, facing homelessness, or just trying to start over.

According to a political brief compiled by the University of Pittsburgh in 2014, sixty-one percent of all poverty in Allegheny County is in the suburbs, a growing trend throughout the United States.[9] These neighbors are often one paycheck away from financial crisis, struggling with money and a deep blanket of shame. Caring community members underwrite Pay It Forward eGift cards (available at the THF register) to assist those wrestling with suburban poverty. When a woman is unable to pay for her selections at Treasure House, a staff member or volunteer says, "Someone who doesn't even know you loves you enough to provide this. Your bill is paid." This statement is often

---

[9] http://d-scholarship.pitt.edu/id/eprint/30488

122 | Course Corrected

received with tears of gratitude. At Treasure House Fashions, women don't have to choose between gas, food, and clothing.

In the past eight years, we've donated approximately $4 million worth of clothing and served more than fifty thousand women. But I'll tell you the truth: It's not about the numbers. It's about the lives. The stories. The healing.

Like the young woman from Ukraine who came in with almost nothing and cried tears of joy as she left with bags of high-quality clothing.

Or the bride whose home and wedding gown were destroyed in a fire days before her wedding, and we helped dress her in a beautiful gown for her special day. Or the high school student whose family couldn't afford a prom dress. She came to us and found three gowns she loved. She selected the perfect one.

These stories matter. These women matter. And every time I hear a new story from a woman who walks through our doors, I remember why I do this.

People sometimes look at me and think I must have it all together. But I've had a very bumpy journey. I've had three marriages, and none of them worked out. I looked at each suitor, and I saw his potential. I saw who he *could* be, not always who he was. And in each marriage, I tried. I fought. I prayed. But the problems were too big—abuse, manipulation, emotional instability—and my own brokenness and bruises contributed to the messes. Nonetheless, I grew into the woman I am today because of each experience and relationship.

From my first marriage, I got my three amazing children, and the impetus to birth Treasure House. From my second, I got the counseling and support I needed to grow mentally and spiritually. From my third, I learned to set boundaries—and that has changed every relationship in my life for the better, *and* I got a bonus daughter who says, "I think the whole reason you were with my dad was so I could have you in my life. You're the best parent I've ever had!"

I always tell women: When lightning strikes once, or more than once, you need to look at where and how you're standing, because regardless of how much damage the lightning caused, you were the lightning rod. What is it in your life that attracts the wrong thing? Did you grow up in a home where women weren't valued? Did you not cultivate a healthy sense of self-worth and self-love? Did you not learn how to set beneficial boundaries? Until you deal with these internal bruises, you'll continue to be the lightning rod, attracting the wrong stuff.

That kind of honest reflection is hard, but it's where healing begins.

I talk to women every week who are hurting. Who feel used up, tossed aside, unseen. And I tell them, "You are *worth* it. You are not the sum of your mistakes or your circumstances. You are a treasure."

Treasure House isn't just for women in crisis; it's for *every* woman. We offer beautiful, high-quality clothing at absurdly affordable prices. And when women shop here—whether they're donating, buying, or just browsing—they're part of something bigger. Their bargains directly support the women who need it most.

And let's be honest—retail therapy is real. But at Treasure House, it comes with dignity, community, and love.

My favorite program is our Sponsored Girls Night Out events. Organizations sponsor groups of women to come shop after hours, enjoy refreshments, and feel celebrated. One night, we hosted women recently released from incarceration. I'll never forget what some of them said:

"This was the best night of my life since leaving jail." "Ms. Sally's talk made me feel like I can do anything." "They made us feel so special. Like we really matter. I guess we do."

Those nights are magical.

But this mission is not just me. It takes a village! I have an incredible team—like Tracy Kincaid, my right hand, who creates order from the chaos, my sister Cindy, who still volunteers at the shop two days a week (or more), and forty volunteers who show up, give big, and love well.

This mission—this calling—was born from the worst time in my life. But it became the best thing that's ever happened to me.

God didn't waste my pain; He transformed it. And now, I get to walk with other women as they do the same.

I started Treasure House Fashions in 2000—twenty-five years ago—when I was fifty years old. The plan was to retire when I turned seventy-five. I've been saying that for several years (much to my board's anxiety). Well, that milestone hits this August, 2025, and I've decided I'm *not retiring*! I love what I do! I love the mission of Treasure House. I'm not done with what I want to accomplish. So, I'm staying!

I recognize I'm at the twilight of my life, but do you know what happens at twilight? You get ready for *fireworks*! This is when *amazing displays* are presented! I've invested blood, sweat, tears, and my personal finances into this mission because I believe in it! I'm not rich and famous, but I am generous. In this divine adventure, my generosity has paid big dividends. I've been honored and blessed to be part of extending the tangible resource of clothing, as well as building self-esteem and *hope* for thousands of women on challenging journeys.

So, if you're walking through something hard—if life feels impossible—hear me when I say this:

There is beauty waiting on the other side of your brokenness. There is purpose in your pain.

God can turn the worst thing into the best thing. I'm living proof. And each day when a woman walks out of Treasure House with a little more joy, a little more confidence, and a little more hope in her heart, I'm reminded this divine adventure is not over yet!

In fact, I think it's just getting good.

Every day, I still get surprised by grace. I still hear stories that stop me in my tracks, that bring me to tears, that remind me why we started in the first place. And I still believe—more than ever—that we are just scratching the surface of what Treasure House can be and do.

We're dreaming again. We're stepping into new possibilities. We're expanding our reach, strengthening partnerships, and building infrastructure to serve even more women with excellence and compassion. We're developing a Workforce

Development Area to equip women not just with clothes, but with confidence, skills, and purpose for their next chapter. We're working toward full accessibility in our store because every woman should feel welcome here. She belongs. Seen. Safe. Celebrated.

That's the heartbeat of Treasure House Fashions.

We're not slowing down—we're gearing up.

Yes, I'm older now. Yes, my hair is grayer (even if the color doesn't expose that!), and my bones creak a little louder than they used to. But my heart? It's young. It's wild. It's burning with purpose. Because I've seen firsthand what hope can do. I've watched it show up in a pair of jeans. In a gown. In a gift card. In a gentle smile or a warm welcome. I've seen it make all the difference.

And I want to keep showing up for that.

So maybe I won't ever fully "retire." Maybe I'll just keep following the holy nudges. Keep listening to the whispers. Keep walking this divine adventure, one sacred step at a time.

Because when you've been rescued from the rubble, when you've seen God take your greatest pain and turn it into your greatest purpose, you can't help but keep going.

And you can't help but cheer for others still finding their way through the dark.

That's what we do at Treasure House. We light the path. We open the doors. We dress women in dignity. We remind them that they are loved, chosen, seen, and *so* much more than their worst day.

So here's my invitation to you—yes, *you*:

If you're in a hard season, don't give up.

If you're healing from heartbreak, keep going.

If you're standing in the ashes, look up. There's beauty on the horizon.

You may not see it yet, but I promise you—it's there. And one day, you'll look back and see how every broken piece was gathered by the hands of a loving God to build something more beautiful than you ever imagined.

I know, because I've lived it.

And I'll keep living it—until my very last breath.
Let's keep rising together.
From the ashes.
Into purpose.
Into hope.
Into the best thing yet.

About Sally

Sally Power is Cinderella turned Fairy Godmother. In 2000, reeling from a painful divorce and left with three children, over $200,000 in debt, and a broken heart, she turned her ashes into action. Out of her own place of desperation, she birthed Treasure House Fashions—a nonprofit women's resale shop with a tender heart and a fierce mission to *promote the dignity and self-esteem of women, particularly those in transition or crisis.*

THF uses the magic of "retail therapy" as a healing balm on bruised souls. Under Sally's spirited leadership, the shop has partnered with over sixty agencies in the Greater Pittsburgh area and served more than fifty thousand women. Since opening its doors, THF has donated more than *$4 million in clothing* in the last eight years.

Sally's life is an ongoing love letter to service. She housed a single mom with twin teens escaping danger, delivered food to families in crisis, mentored women launching their own nonprofits, and cried alongside grieving mothers. Before founding THF, she spent thirty-six years as a teacher of Deaf and hard-of-hearing students and provided sign language interpretation in numerous faith-based settings.

A self-proclaimed "hot mess," Sally insists her *mess has become her message*. She doesn't pretend to have it all together. Instead, she offers honesty, humor, and hope—encouraging women not to be defined by their pain or past, but to press forward knowing that *faith, perseverance, and maybe even a fairy godmother* can work it all together for good.

Her impact has been recognized through more than a dozen awards, including Circle of Courage, Western PA Gamechanger, KDKA Hometown Hero, Get Involved Person of the Year (2023), and Powered by Purpose from Curio 412 (2023). Her story was even featured in *Woman's Day Magazine* (May 2010), though Sally insists it was her "ugliest photo and ugliest outfit ever!" She laughs, "I'm cuter now and have better clothes. Please run an update!" The national recognition was humbling—but also inspiring.

Sally may not be rich or famous, but she is *undeniably generous*. She's invested blood, sweat, tears, and her personal finances into a mission that has turned tragedy into triumph for thousands of women.

Stop by Treasure House Fashions at 7607 McKnight Road, Pittsburgh, PA 15237. Whether you come to shop, donate, or discover your own bit of magic, one thing's for sure—you'll leave reminded that *you are a treasure*.

Connect with Sally
www.thfashions.org

Breaking the Chains, Finding the Light

Denise Stiffler

Have you ever felt as though you were living under a dark cloud? Even on a really good day, it seems clouds are still covering the sun. You can't shake the nagging feeling that things in your life are off, but you are unable to put your finger on what is wrong or what could be happening to you.

That was me for a decade of my adult life. As a child, I was always the bubbly girl. Little and big things alike brought me joy. I cherished my friendships and family members. I could empathize well with others. I would always find some good in every circumstance, and even my worst days had some form of sunshine in them.

Things began to change as I got older. I started noticing a shift in me early on in my marriage. My excitement level for things was down. I was constantly questioning myself. I would have random little bursts of fear as I was in the midst of day-to-day tasks: *Oh shoot, did I put the garage door down?* or *I hope I turned the Crock-Pot on or dinner won't be ready when I get home.* When these bursts of fear came up, I felt paralyzed, as if I had made a grave mistake. I constantly doubted myself, living in fear, and felt stripped of the joy I naturally carried for so long. I wouldn't realize it until years later, but all of this fear and stress were directly correlated with my marriage.

These struggles intensified as I became a mother. When my first daughter was born, some of the relationships that I held dear for most of my life began to strain. I started keeping my distance from people, as if they weren't safe. I never feared for my or my daughter's life, nor did I suffer from postpartum depression, but it seemed these random fears morphed into false belief systems that told me to keep my struggles to myself. I believed people would judge me for the struggles I was facing at home as a mother and wife.

This went on for years. I became a stay-at-home mom when my oldest was one and a half years old, and the next year, my second daughter was born. Being home with them, while joyful, didn't alleviate any of the fears and beliefs I was carrying. My husband worked long hours every day of the week and sometimes weekends, so it was just me and my daughters most of the time. I was incredibly lonely. I never felt as though I measured up, and parenting solo was challenging some days.

After about five years of staying home with my girls, I could sense something was very, very off in my marriage. My husband had recently discovered streaming games and was spending a lot of time in his office at night instead of our typical time together after the girls went to bed.

One night, I remember hearing him laughing in his office while I tossed and turned in bed, unable to sleep. I eventually got out of bed, knocked on the door, and told him to come out and explain what was happening with us. He had been so distant lately, and I couldn't figure out why. He told me he was no longer in love with me and wanted out of our marriage.

The rejection was swift and cut like a knife. I had no idea what to make of it. How does a marriage just end so abruptly with no warning? We had just celebrated a wedding anniversary the week prior. I felt sick to my stomach and had a hard time breathing.

Did I sense we had a good marriage? No. However, thanks to my ability to find the bright spot in every situation, I was constantly telling myself that we were in a hard season being parents to two young children, and we would find a way. Every marriage goes through challenging seasons, right? He, however, did not see it that way.

After he told me this, I definitely couldn't sleep. I remember late that same night, I walked down the stairs to our living room, and my whole body was shaking as if releasing all the weight and fear I had been carrying for the last decade. My joy had been squashed down to barely anything and I was constantly questioning my worth, wondering if I was doing and being enough. Even though my life had done a complete 180-degree turn in a matter of moments, my body began to exhale everything I had been carrying.

The next day, I called my best friend, whom I've known since we were babies. I talked, wept, and laid it all out. I was no longer going to live in fear of others' judgment. I refused to walk this new path alone. I called another one of my closest friends, and I will remember her words to me forever. She said, "You're a lot to lose." I needed to be reminded of my worth, and her words were a balm to my soul that day.

While having support didn't fix all the problems, I now knew the light could start to come back in. Over the course of a year and a half, I adjusted to having mostly sole custody of my children while my husband and I were separated and went through the divorce process. I also dove head-first into therapy and building a healthier mindset and habits, leaned in to family and friends, and started to feel as though the light and joy were going to come back in.

All of that came to a screeching halt right before I signed the divorce papers. My soon-to-be ex-husband sent me an email detailing that he had been seeing someone. She, along with her two young children, would be moving in with him in a few weeks. Prior to this, I was led to believe he would be living alone. This was a complete blindside. (It should be noted that when we sat down to divide assets and talk about custody, we handled things amicably).

Upon reading this news, my entire body went numb. I had a hard time breathing. It is one thing to be left so abruptly; it is another thing entirely to be betrayed. I started connecting the dots and realized he had been talking to her before he left our marriage. He had flown out to see her multiple times during our separation, even spending holidays with her.

At this point in the journey, I had just begun to feel as though the light at the end of the tunnel was getting closer, only to be thrown back into total darkness. I wanted to sit down and talk with him about how our children were entering a new family unit with him in a matter of weeks. I wanted to better understand what this new normal would be like for them since I was led to believe it would look very different prior to this. I was told anything I wanted to say could be said in an email. He had no interest in talking with me.

It didn't make sense to me. How could someone relay all of this information, knowing it would deeply hurt me, and then avoid me afterward and not let me speak my piece? There was no apology. A few weeks later, he would text me to tell me his girlfriend was also pregnant. All of the hiding he had been doing was finally coming to light.

In the months following this, I discovered betrayal upon betrayal, causing me to question if those who supported my ex were intentionally trying to hurt me. After learning about the infidelity, I realized his parents were driving him to the airport multiple times throughout the year to see her. It was as though he and his family were playing nice, but keeping secrets only hurt me more.

The first time I saw his parents after our divorce was final, they pretended I wasn't there while they played with the new children. These were people who promised they would always love me, and I would always be their daughter. Suddenly, those words were empty. It was as though I was the black sheep in a situation entirely created by all of them.

These moments, and so many others, radically shifted healing for me. Before all of this happened, the healing that took place involved changing my mindset, but if I was ever going to see the light again, I had deep soul work to do.

When this journey abruptly began, the one thing I knew I wanted was to be able to walk with my head held high and make decisions from a confident, empowered place. My therapist would constantly ask me in our sessions, "What would a wise, strong, confident woman do?"

In therapy, we did multiple sessions of EMDR (eye movement desensitization and reprocessing), which is described as "a mental health treatment technique. This method involves moving your eyes a specific way while you process traumatic memories. EMDR's goal is to help you heal from trauma or other distressing life experiences."[10] In one of these sessions, I remember seeing myself chained to the ocean floor. Every time I tried to swim to shore, I would get yanked back down. During that session, I saw myself yanking my ankle out of the chains and coming up for air. It was a turning point for me. A symbol of how I was no longer going to stay stuck, not by my old thought patterns and beliefs, and not by those who were causing me pain. Regardless of how I had been treated, I didn't have to continue to let others rob me of joy, hope, love, and everything good I believed in, yet had lost along the way.

I've always been a person of faith, and leaning into scripture and my relationship with God kept me stable and helped me find the light again. There are so many instances in the Bible where God's people had been betrayed, left, and felt alone. Even Jesus Himself was betrayed! This was a reminder that God never wastes our pain, and no matter how dark things seemed, there were faith giants before me who got through their hard seasons.

I would never wish the pain and betrayal I've experienced on my worst enemy. However, through healing, I've come to realize that life can still be beautiful. I don't have to live in fear. I don't have to hide. I can have joy and excitement abundantly. The light shines in now; the darkness doesn't win anymore.

I will never forget the first time I knew I was going to survive everything and be OK. My daughters and I drove to Florida to spend Christmas with family. I always enjoy a good road trip, yet I was nervous driving this long way by myself without any backup or help with the kids. Turns out, I didn't need help. The three of us had a blast. When we crossed the state line into Florida, it was sunny and warm. We rolled the windows down, blasted music, and sang at the top of our lungs. I knew at that moment life was going to be beautiful again.

---

[10] https://my.clevelandclinic.org/health/treatments/22641-emdr-therapy

The more I've healed, the more I've learned that my story is not an uncommon one. It breaks my heart to see women and men in situations where they are constantly shrinking and living an unfulfilling life. So many people are suffering in silence because they can't quite put their finger on what is happening to them. They become shells of themselves over time. It's been my honor to walk alongside others as a life coach and help them unpack these challenging realities. The journey is messy and gritty at times, but the result is beautiful and worth it.

It is worthwhile to ask ourselves every so often, *Is this the life I want to be living*? If the answer to that is yes, then by all means, keep doing what you are doing. Yet if there is even the slightest pause in that answer, it is worth taking stock of your life and seeing where you are out of alignment. If you are a person of faith, are you fulfilling the life you feel called to or are you allowing fear to hold you back? Do you feel off and can't quite figure out what is going on? I encourage you to seek counsel on these things. It helps to have an outside perspective to offer guidance and ask you the right questions as you navigate a deeper understanding of yourself.

One of the best parts of my life now is that I have a peaceful and joyful home. My daughters and I have dance parties all the time. My family relationships and friendships have been restored. I have a fulfilling career helping others. I don't hide the hard parts of my life anymore because I don't feel ashamed of them. When fear creeps in, I've learned that I can feel the fear, and it doesn't have to derail me. I don't have to shame myself for these feelings or for being forgetful. I can offer myself grace and love and talk to myself like I would my best friend. The voices of criticism, while they still come because I'm human, aren't the main narrative anymore, and for that I am grateful.

What is it you most desire for your life? While I can't promise healing will always be pretty, I can promise one day you will get to a place where you have fulfillment in your life. Peace and joy will exist in your life in ways you didn't think were possible before. Have hope and let the light in!

About Denise

Denise Stiffler is a dedicated mom, inspiring speaker, podcast cohost, author, and passionate advocate for women's healing. As cohost of the empowering podcast, *From Run Down to Renewed*, she helps offer insight, encouragement, and practical tools for transformation and hope for women as they dive deeper into their faith. She also shares her journey and expertise with authenticity and compassion as a sought-after speaker at women's conferences and events.

As a certified life coach, Denise specializes in helping women heal from toxic and harmful relationships. Through her coaching, she empowers women to reclaim their worth, rediscover their voice, and step into the fulfilling life they deserve. Her mission is clear: to guide women out of survival mode and into a life of purpose, confidence, and joy.

Connect with Denise
http://linktr.ee/denise.lifecoach7

Conclusion

Cori Wamsley

The lesson from this book is a simple one: relax and don't try to white knuckle everything. You're on the right path, at the right time, even if it feels like everything is turning upside down.

And the funny thing is that so many of us will need to learn this lesson time and again because, ultimately, we want that control. We want to think that we know better. And yet, if we watch for the little things, the nudges or signs or whatever you want to call them, we get confirmation that this is what we are supposed to be doing or something better is in store.

Our paths are never a straight line but more like the track for a roller coaster with curves and flips and sometimes unexpected standstills.

When we're younger, though, our expectations are more like a checklist, like there is something we do to get to the obvious next thing, to get to the obvious thing after that, and on and on. The first time I had an inkling that this wasn't normal was when I was in middle school and several kids at my table in home ec were talking about what their parents did for a living. It's a conversation I'll never forget.

One of my friends, Chris, said that his dad was a mailman, but he had been something else before that and another thing before that. He named off half a dozen things that his dad had done while Chris was growing up, and he was met unexpectedly with laughter from several of the other kids at the table.

"Your dad is a loser who can't keep a job," one of the boys spat out. I remember feeling so much pain for Chris in that moment as the laughter echoed around us.

But out of nowhere, our teacher cut everyone off with, "Sounds like someone with a lot of interests who loves trying new things." The silence that followed as the energy in that room flipped was glorious.

Not only did she protect Chris in the cleverest way possible, but she also gave us all permission to follow our own paths, showing us that there isn't judgment for that, or that there shouldn't be. I don't remember much about middle school over thirty years later, but that moment stands out in my mind any time it seems like someone, even me, is having a tough time keeping to "the plan."

I believe that the women in this book will nod in agreement when they read this, as we've all taken twisting paths, sometimes backtracking, sometimes jumping from a moving car onto a train going in the opposite direction, but always listening to our hearts, our guts, our guides when it's time to move.

This is one reason why we chose to support the mission of Treasure House Fashions of Pittsburgh, Pa., with proceeds from this book. Treasure House Fashions is a nonprofit, quality women's resale clothing shop with a boutique-style atmosphere, acting as the "closet" for over sixty agencies in the greater Pittsburgh area. While anyone can shop there, Treasure House partners with organizations where women often turn when they need a little extra help, and the authors of *Course Corrected* honor their new uncharted courses with this book.

If you're curious about Treasure House Fashions or would like to donate to their cause, please visit their website at www.thfashions.org.

And remember that you are in control of your choices as you navigate the choppy waters of being a human, but ultimately, we all end up where we are meant to be, and that makes the journey that much sweeter!

About Cori Wamsley

Award-winning author Cori Wamsley, CEO of Aurora Corialis Publishing, works with leaders who have a transformational story to share. She helps them quickly and easily write and publish a book for their brand that helps them create a legacy and be seen as an expert while building a relationship with the reader. She also hosted the livestream podcast Page-Turner's Studio with Cori.

Cori has 20 years' experience as a professional writer and editor, including 10 years with the Departments of Energy and Justice and four years as the executive editor of *Inspiring Lives Magazine*.

Cori has written eleven fiction books and one nonfiction book, *The SPARK Method: How to Write a Book for Your Business Fast*, and contributed to two anthologies. Her book *Braving the Shore* won first place in fiction at The Author Zone Awards in 2023, and Cori was a nominee for the Brave Women Project's Evolve Pillar Award the same year. Her book *The Treasures We Seek* won first place in fiction at The Author Zone Awards in 2024, and her book *Good in Theory* won third place in women's fiction at The BookFest Awards in 2025.

Connect with Cori

www.auroracorialispublishing.com

www.coriwamsley.com

https://www.facebook.com/cori.smithwamsley/

https://www.instagram.com/coriwamsley_author/

https://www.tiktok.com/@coriwamsleyauthor

https://www.pinterest.com/soulsisterhoodseries/

www.ingramcontent.com/pod-product-compliance
Lightning Source LLC
Chambersburg PA
CBHW071152120626
46546CB00006B/2225